AUTOBIOGRAPHY OF AN ELDERLY WOMAN

Published @ 2017 Trieste Publishing Pty Ltd

ISBN 9780649069026

Autobiography of an Elderly Woman by Mary Heaton Vorse

Edited by Trieste Publishing Pty Ltd.
Cover @ 2017

www.triestepublishing.com

MARY HEATON VORSE

AUTOBIOGRAPHY OF AN ELDERLY WOMAN

Trieste

AUTOBIOGRAPHY

OF

AN ELDERLY WOMAN

" As soon as you feel too old to do a thing,
do it." — Margaret Deland.

BOSTON AND NEW YORK

HOUGHTON MIFFLIN COMPANY

1911

AUTOBIOGRAPHY OF AN
ELDERLY WOMAN

Published September 1911

CONTENTS

AUTOBIOGRAPHY OF AN ELDERLY WOMAN

CHAPTER I

THE SHADOW OF AGE

As I look back over my life, it divides itself into four parts. First come all the years before I married, and as I look back on my childhood and my short girlhood, it seems to me as though I were remembering the life of some other woman, for during these many years I know that I have changed several times from one person to another, and the world about me has had time to change also. All that early part swims in a fog, with here and there events popping out of the mist, more distinct than those a week past, — often meaningless and

1

trivial events these; I cannot tell by what caprice memory has elected to keep them so clear. Lately I find myself returning to certain opinions and prejudices of my girlhood, that I had long forgotten. Time, after all, has not obliterated them, nor have I walked away from them. It is rather as though I had gone in a circle, and as I come to the completion of it I find my old thoughts and opinions, changed and grown older, waiting for me.

With my marriage begins the part of my life that seems real to me, — it is as if I had dreamed all that went before. I loved the time when my children were little, and I have often wished that I could put them and myself back in the nursery again. I pity the women whose children come too late for them

all to be in some sense children together. But however young a mother
is, there is a great gap between her
and her babies. My little children were
of a different generation from me. And
for all our striving to understand, they
were babies and my husband and I
"grown people," though as I look back
we seem mere boy and girl.

We worried over our babies, — there
were four of them, all in the nursery
at the same time, — we sat up nights
gravely discussing their "tendencies,"
and their education — only to find that
the very tendencies over which we
worried most they outgrew, and that
when the time for education began in
earnest, all the conditions had changed
and new methods had been evolved.

It will always be this way, — mothers

8

and fathers will always sit up late nights, as we did, discussing the "futures" of their little two-year-old sons.

We tried so hard to do right; we thought back through the years and said:—

"I felt this and this when I was little. I thought this way and this—such and such things frightened me. My father seemed unjust when he punished me for this offense; my mother made such and such mistakes. I will not make these mistakes with my children."

And so, thinking to avoid all the mistakes of our own parents, we made, all unknowing, fresh mistakes of our own.

When I was little, for instance, I was very much afraid of the dark; so much so that the fears of my childhood

4

haunted my whole life, — an unlighted staircase has terrors for me even to this day. And I made up my mind that no child of mine should suffer from fear of darkness as I did. So my first child had a light in his room. He was always naughty about going to bed, and he grew to be a big boy before I found out that this was because the gray twilight of the room was horrible to him, and that he was very much afraid of the uncertain shapes of the furniture he saw in the dim light of the lamp, though not at all afraid of the dark. It is with such well-intentioned blunders that one brings up one's children.

Grandmothers know that this is so, and for that reason all the various "systems" seem like foolish words to them. They have learned that there will be mistakes made where there are parents and children, — yes, and that there will be cruelties and injustices, and that the only way to deal with very little children is to love them very much and let them feel this love.

The time my children took in growing up seems to me phenomenally short; one day they were babies and the next they were young people to be reckoned with, having wills and personalities of their own. Other mothers tell me that their children grew up as quickly, but this I have hard work to believe.

When my oldest son was nearly a man and the others crowding on his heels, my dear husband died, and my son grew up overnight, and in the next few years — years that were very full ones,

6

for all their sadness — my other children stole a march on me and grew up too; almost, I might say, behind my back. While I was taking on myself the new responsibilities of my so altered life, and while the world seemed yet very empty of companionship, I found that my children were becoming my comrades, and so I entered on the third quarter of my life.

My boys and girls all at once belonged to my generation; we had common interests, common tastes and amusements — for all practical purposes we were the same age. It was at this time that the warning voice sounded in my ear, but I seemed to myself almost as young as my children, so no wonder I did n't recognize it as the voice of age calling to me. It is a very pleasant time

7

when one is still on the great stage of life, playing one's small part shoulder to shoulder with one's children ; shoulder to shoulder, too, with people a score of years one's senior. This is the golden moment when time holds its breath for a while and one imagines that, however old one may get, one will forever stay in spirit at the same smiling "middle way." Age, considered at that time, seems rather the result of some accident or some weakness of will than the result of living a great number of years in the world. So for many years my children and I did our work side by side, I helping and advising them, they aiding and advising me in the common partnership of our lives.

The fourth part of my life, my present life about which I am going to

write, began when again I became of a
different generation from my children
— with the difference that they now
are the strong, I the weak ; that they
treasure me and care for me, worry
over me and weep over me, — a spry
old lady, and, I am afraid, sometimes
a defiant old lady, impatient of the rules
which they lay down for me, as once
they were of the rules that I made for
them.

How did this come about ? When
did it happen ?

There was a time when I was more
of a comrade than a mother to my
daughters ; when I was the adviser of
my sons. Now I am not. I do not know
when the change came, nor do they, if
indeed they realize it at all. There was
a time when I was of their generation,

9

now I am not. I cannot put my finger on the time when old age finally claimed me. But there came a moment when my boys were more thoughtful of me, when they did n't come to me any more with their perplexities, not because I had what is called "failed," but because they felt that the time had come when I ought to be "spared" every possible worry. So there is a conspiracy of silence against me in my household. "We must n't worry mother," is the watchword of my dear children, and the result of their great care is that I am on the outside of their lives.

Shadows come and go among them; they talk about them; I feel the chill of their trouble, but I 'm never told what it 's about. Before me they keep cheerful; when I come, the shadow

passes from their faces and they talk
with me about all the things that they
think will interest me. I move in a little
artificial, smiling world away from all
the big interests of life. If one of them
is sick away from home, I am not told
until it is all over ; if there is any crisis
among them, they do all they can to
keep me from hearing of it. But in the
end I always do know, for no one can
live in the shadow of any anxiety and
not be aware of it.

So the great silence enfolds me more
and more. I live more alone and solitary among those I love, groping in the
silence, watching the faces of my children to find what is passing in their
lives. I often think how sweet it would
have been if my husband had lived, and
we could have grown old together,

11

understanding and giving companionship to each other.

I can remember the very day when I *realized* that age had claimed me at last. There is a great difference between being a thing and realizing it. A woman may say a hundred times that she is ugly ; she may be ugly ; but unless she realizes that she is ugly, it will make very little difference. It is the consciousness of our defects which undoes us,— and so with age.

This great readjustment began with the most trivial of events. I happened to see a little dust on the table and around on the bric-a-brac — it seems to me that dusting is a lost art — and I was just wiping it off. I was enjoying myself, for I belong to a generation which was taught to work with its

12

hands and to delight in doing its work nicely, when I heard Margaret's step on the stairs; she is my youngest daughter, home on a visit. My first impulse was to sit down and pretend to be reading, but I resolved to brazen it out, — after all, there is no reason why I shouldn't dust my own bric-a-brac in my own home if I choose.

She came into the parlor.

" *What* are you doing, darling?" she said.

"I am dusting the vases on the mantel," I answered, and I tried to keep any note of guilt from my voice.

"Why couldn't you have called Annie?" she asked me, with tender reproach.

" I like to stir around myself some-

18

times," I said, and for the life of me I couldn't help being a little defiant.

"Well, then, why couldn't you let me do it? You might have called me," she went on in the same tone.

"I told you I like to do it."

"It isn't good for you to stand on your feet so much. Give me that duster, mother. You'll tire yourself all out."

"I get tired *sitting*," I broke out.

"I always have said that you ought to take more exercise in the open air." By this time she had taken away my duster. "Why don't you go out and take a little walk? Come — I'll go with you."

Presently she had finished dusting, but I saw ever so many little places that I should have to wipe up later on, fur-

14

tively. I should have enjoyed finishing that dusting myself.

"I'll run up and get your things," said Margaret.

Now, I cannot abide having any one trifle with my bureau drawers, and it is n't because I 'm old enough to have middle-aged sons and daughters, either. Ever since I can remember, I have put my things away myself. I keep my bonnets in the little drawers and my gloves and veils—my everyday ones, that is—beside them; and I know that I shall never be able to find anything again once Margaret has been among them. Besides that, I do not like going to walk. Walking aimlessly for exercise has always seemed most futile to me; a feeble stroll that has no objective point, not even the post office, annoys me more than any other way of spending my time. I have never walked except when I had something to walk for, and I don't intend to begin at my time of life.

"I don't think I'll go to walk, dear. I'm going out this afternoon —"

Now, though I said this indifferently enough, in a tone which didn't invite discussion, yet I braced myself inwardly; I knew what was coming.

" Oh, mother darling," my daughter cried. " You're not going to that lecture, with your cold, in that drafty hall ! And you always catch more cold in a crowd ! You won't go, will you?"

" Well, well — " I temporized.

" You won't go — promise."

Then the door-bell rang, and I made my escape to my own room and locked

16

my door after me. I knew well enough what would happen, — how Margaret would tell the others at dinner that I was going out, and how they would protest. And I made up my mind, as I often have before, that since I am old enough to know what is best for me, I would go to that lecture, let them talk as they might; so I got ready for the battle, resolving for the hundredth time that I would not be run by my children.

As I sat in my room plotting — yes, plotting — how I should outwit my daughter, it came over me what a funny thing it was that I should be contriving to get my own way, for all the world like a naughty, elderly child, while my daughter was worrying about my headstrong ways as if

17

she were my mother instead of my being hers.

How increasingly often I hear as the years go on, not only from my own children, but from other people whose mothers are already old: "Mother will not take care of herself!" And then follow fearsome stories of mother's latest escapade, — just as one tells how naughty Johnnie is getting and how Susie kicks her bedclothes off, — stories of how mother made a raid on the attic and cleaned it almost single-handed when all the family were away; stories of clandestine descents into the perilous depths of the cellar; hair-raising tales of how mother was found on a stepladder hanging a window curtain; how mother insisted on putting down the preserves and pickles, — rows and

rows and rows of shining glasses of
them, — herself, and how tired she was
afterwards, as if putting down the preserves tired only women who were past
middle age. And a certain indignation
rose within me as I remembered that
I can visit my own attic and my own
cellar only by stealth or with a devoted
and tyrannical child of mine standing
over me to see that I don't "overdo."
For the motto of all devoted sons and
daughters is: "Nag mother to death,
if necessary, but don't let her overdo."

Well, what if I should overdo? Before one is old, one is allowed to shorten
one's life unchecked; one may have
orgies of work undisturbed. And I, for
one, would far rather shorten my life
by overdoing than have it lengthened
out by a series of mournful, inactive

19

years. Again I said I would not be run by my children. And as I got to this point in my meditation I heard my son Dudley coming up the stairs. I knew he would come to see me, so I unlocked my door.

I had said that I would not be run by my children. Now see to what depths constant nagging reduces a naturally straightforward woman. I know that Dudley watches me very closely, and I often wish he would sometimes ignore my moods as I do his; but this time I was ready for him, pulling a long face when he came in.

He said at once—I knew he would:—

"You look blue, old girl."

"I never," I burst out, "can do the least thing without you children interfering. I can't read *all* the time, you know; but whenever I propose to do anything, I meet with such opposition that for the sake of peace I give up at once."

I spoke more warmly than I felt as far as this particular instance was concerned, for I was fighting for a principle.

"Who's been bothering you?" Dudley demanded.

"It isn't 'bothered' I've been," I remonstrated. "It's that you children are needlessly anxious about me. It's far better for me to go out now and then than to sit in the house from morning till night. And what's more," I added determinedly, "I am going to the lecture this afternoon no matter what Margaret or any one else says!"

Dudley laughed.

21

"There, there," he said, patting my hand. "You *shall* go; no one is going to oppose you. You'll go if I have to take you there in a carriage myself."

So I knew I had won the day, for in our family Dudley is the important member. But I made up my mind, just the same, that I would go on my own two feet to that lecture, for there was no need at all of a carriage. And I did go, alone and walking, though I slipped out of the front door so quietly that it was hardly dignified, — "sneaked," was what Margaret called it.

As Dudley went down the hall, I thought how a similar warfare is being carried on all over this country to-day, wherever there are elderly mothers and middle-aged sons and daughters, — the children trying to dominate their parents with the end in view of making them take abnormal care of their health, and the older people fighting ever more feebly and petulantly for their lost independence. Not only struggling to have their own way, not only chafing at the leading-strings in which their watchful, devoted children would keep them, but fighting, too, for the little glimmer of youth that is yet left them.

For all this care by one's children means but one thing, and that is — age. While you slept, old age came upon you. You count the number of your years by the way your daughter watches your steps, and you see your infirmities in your son's anxious eyes; and the reason of all this struggle — why our own attics and cellars are forbidden ground to us; why our daugh-

23

ters take our dusters from us and tenderly nag us — is that they are valiantly, if tactlessly, striving to delay by their care the hour which they know must come, while we try to ignore its approach.

We like to kill the days, which sometimes crawl past us so slowly, with an illusion of activity, and we do not like to be reminded day by day, hour by hour, that we are old, that there is no work we need do, no "ought" calling us any more; that our work in the world is being done by other people and our long vacation has already begun.

As I sat alone that evening and soberly went over the events of the day, I clearly realized the meaning of Margaret's taking away my duster. I real-

ized that there was no work in the
world that I ought to do but take care
of myself. I realized that I was old,
and from that day, though I often forget it, the world has looked a little different to me; my point of view has, in
some subtle way, shifted. It was on
that day that I sat down to think how
it was that I had come to be old and
what the invisible milestones were that
I had passed along the way.

The first time age touched me it was
with so light a finger that I did not recognize the touch; I did n't know what
had happened. Indeed, the touch of age
at first irritated me; then I laughed at
it, and finally I became a little bewildered,
realizing confusedly that a new ele-
ment had come into my life to stay. But
I did not know that it was the shadow

25

of age which was upon me, that it was always there, invisible, quiet, persistent, and, patient as death, waiting to claim me.

This first touch of age comes when our children begin to dictate to us.

The other day I saw the youth of a woman begin to wither under my very eyes. She did n't know what was happening, but I knew what shadow was over her. To me she seems young, for I have seen her grow up, and though she has big daughters, I never thought of her as approaching middle age until the last time she and the girls came to see me.

Edith is a big, handsome, buoyant woman, but there was a subdued air about her for which I could n't account until her eldest daughter said sweetly, but with decision : —

"Mother isn't looking well; she ought to have some sea air."

And Edith replied with the note of helpless irritation that I have come to know so well : —

"I have told the children so often that I dislike leaving my comfortable home in the summer."

Then I knew why Edith seemed changed : her children had begun to run her.

So the finger of age touches all of us in much the same fashion. The warning may not always come through some dear child, though with mothers it is oftenest in that way ; but the voice of the valiant new generation speaks in one way or another to every man and woman, and from the moment you have heard that voice you have set your face old-agewards, though twenty years or more may pass before you are really old. The strong new generation, eager and clamorous, is at your heels ready to take your place, anxious to perform your tasks. Already your children are altering the world that you know; already they are meditating the changes that they will make when the reins of power fall into their hands; and one day you will wake up in a new world, an unhomelike place to which you must adjust yourself as a baby must adjust himself to his surroundings, but with the difference that every day the baby makes progress, whereas every day you will find the new conditions harder to understand, — as I have, and as your mother has.

After my husband's death I was very

anxious to have my own mother make her home with me, and at the time I could n't understand why she would n't. Now I know. She lived instead in a little house in the town where she had spent her life, and for all companionship she had a " girl " nearly as old as herself. We used to worry about her a great deal, about her loneliness, her lack of care of herself, — all the things that my children worry about now ; but she met all our pleading to live with us with the baffling smile, and the " Well, well, we 'll see," that she had used with us when we were little children.

One time I accompanied her home after a visit she had made us, in spite of her protests that it was ridiculous for me to do so. It had stormed and the roads were bad, and I was afraid to let

her travel alone. She strode ahead of
me, straight as a pine tree, up the brick
path which led to her house, and opened
the front door. The gesture of welcome
she gave her lonely little home, and the
long breath she drew, as of relief, I
didn't then understand, though I always remembered them. I understand
now. She had come back to herself, to
her own life, to her memories. Here she
could think her own thoughts and lead
her life as she wished. She could even
sit in a draft without an affectionately officious child following her up
with a shawl, and her little home, lonely
as it was, was less lonely than the strange
world we lived in. I have often taken
the duster from my mother's hands as
Margaret did from mine the other morning. And I suppose the same little

drama will be enacted in every family until the end of time by mothers and daughters.

CHAPTER II

MY MOTHER'S HOUSE

As my years crowd upon me, I read the meaning of certain things in the past that as a young woman I never understood, for there is nothing more variable than our past. Young people regard the happenings of yesterday as a fixed quantity, but the past is just as insecure as the future, for all events have meaning and gather value only according to the personality they visit. This being so, as time changes, the tragedy of yesterday softens and smiles at one. The small and meaningless event, in the light of those which follow it, grows and grows until it overshadows all.

The boundaries that fix life itself — birth and death — are perhaps the only events that keep their primary importance with us as we age. Mysterious is the past and strange and fortuitous. It veils its face like the future. We cannot remember what we will ; we forget the very things that we have loved and felt and suffered. The memory of the emotions passes from us, and it is as if they had never been. Why should I keep this trivial memory and discard the other? Who can tell me? I know that this and that, when I was a girl, made my heart beat; this I remember, but not with my emotions. Why it beat is now mysterious to me.

As I grow old I find myself in a thousand looks and gestures of my mother, the memories of which come crowding to me out of the past. We go down to the grave as egotists ; so it is the mother of her later years who now returns to me as I tread over the path she trod.

Especially significant is her house,— the little place so liberally fenced in and not thrown into the next place in the modern and odious fashion. Up the side of the brick path were posy beds, — for that is the true name for such a garden, — and posy beds there were in front of the house, and behind grew other flowers. These my mother tended herself; the lawn was cared for by a gardener. This man was a great thorn in the side of all of us who visited her. He spent his days gossiping cheerily over the fence, telling the neighbors details like the difference between the ther-

mometer in the shade and in the sun.
He would communicate to them at what
hour he had arisen that morning and how
his hens were laying. His cheerful and
ceaseless babble went on whenever he
found an ear to receive it. This old man
annoyed us, as I said. He was a kindly
soul, and we had no objection to him as
an individual, but his prattle bored us,
and we felt that he should work for the
stipend he received for mowing the lawn
and raking up the leaves. This feeling
our mother did not share; she was contented to let him dawdle through the
hours of the day if he chose, so that
some time or other the lawn was cut;
and as she pottered about her flowers,
gloves on her hands and a wide shade
hat on her head — for she was of the
generation whose gentlewomen were

taught to be careful of their complexion and their hands, and thought it unbecoming in a delicate female to get blowzy with sunburn and blackened with tan — she would stop and talk with him.

We would point out to her that she was encouraging him in his idle habits, and were always ready at a moment's notice to furnish her with a strong likely boy of eighteen in place of this doddering and garrulous individual. I can remember conversations like this : —

"Mother, I've heard that Widow Johnson's boy wants to work — "

" Widow Johnson's boy! That weedy bean-pole — all legs ! "

" He 's eighteen — "

"I know your eighteen-year-olds," my mother would cry. "They stop working the moment your back is turned. I like my man; I can depend on him."

"Yes," we would reply bitterly, "you can depend on him to do nothing. Besides, you'll be helping the boy's mother."

We knew that a practice of my mother's was to help along solitary women less fortunately placed than she had been.

But to this suggestion she would reply with a masterful definiteness : —

"I'm not an eleemosynary institution, my dear."

There was no arguing with her; there was no making her see that that was precisely what she was. There was no use offering her men in the prime of life to mow her lawn any more than there was in offering her what she called "tittering and hooting boys."

She was just as bad about the bits of carpentry that there were to be done around the house. There was a certain workman who came occasionally on odd jobs and whom we tried to have her get rid of, but for whom, after all, we had a sneaking fondness.

I can remember this old man well. He seemed no thicker than a piece of paper and gave the impression of some odd ghost, so bent-over was he, so pale, — a strange, tanned pallor, framed in by tenuous hair and sparse, white whiskers. He moved brokenly and feebly, and yet clung with the tenacity of a fly to the side of a roof. He liked shingling, he said; it kept him young.

This I doubt, nor have I ever yet tried it for the disease of age.

My mother claimed he was a good carpenter. That may have been ; at any rate, all the carpentering that was done, was done by him, from shingling to pottering over a broken piazza rail. What especially irritated us about him was that his memory had departed from him. It was impossible for him to remember for ten consecutive minutes where to find his tools. One could find him at any unexpected place, always, he said, looking for the nails or the screwdriver or the hammer. He strewed them about him with as lavish a gesture as Millet's Sower, so one might judge from the length of time he spent looking for them. He would wander from room to room, peering with nearsighted eyes

89

into every corner; and sometimes he
would forget which tool it was he had
lost, and would have to go back to find
out, and then begin the search all over
again. He never became impatient at
this, but continued his long wanderings
like some little New England "Wandering Jew," in sorrow over the unnatural
perversity of his tools rather than in
any anger against them.

A third person my mother employed
of this same kind; this one a painter.
He was elderly also; garrulous, but in
a different way from the childlike prattle of the gardener.

No, he couldn't tell how much a
thing would cost. Perhaps it would cost
so much, and perhaps so much; he
couldn't tell until he got through. No,
he couldn't tell you how long it would

take him, — perhaps a day, perhaps
longer; — he did n't know. When would
he come? He did n't know; maybe
to-morrow, — maybe next day, — he
could n't tell.

"But," my mother would persist,
"we 've got to have that kitchen floor
painted and we 've got to know when
you 're coming, Mr. Bunner."

"Well, now, Mis' Paine, I can't tell
you. Now, I 'll tell you how it is; I 'm
waitin' now for some paint to paint
Malcolm's house, an' when I get that
paint, I 'll paint his house, an' when I
get that done, I 'll do your kitchen."

"But while you 're waiting," my
mother would urge.

And you can imagine us fairly tramp-
ing up and down with rage, wishing to
poke forth from the doors the old piker.

41

And thus it would go on, and after spending more or less of kindliness on him, my mother would at last persuade the old man to come the next day.

As I look back on it, it seems as if always one or the other of these feckless elderly workmen was engaged in doing some odd job or other around my mother's place, and I think this was very likely true. I know now why she did it; it gave her that feeling with which we older people like to deceive ourselves, — and succeed according to the clearness of our mental capacity, — the illusion of activity, of really accomplishing something; and my mother accomplished this: that she kept up her house spick and span to her last moment. I know now, too, why she had these elderly people about her, and why she couldn't abide the smart, modern methods of younger and more efficient people. Not only had they worked for her for years and she had a loyalty towards her own generation, but I think she had some deeper sympathy and liking for their failing powers. Possibly she saw her own mirrored in theirs; perhaps she remembered when the old carpenter was as spry as a kitten and when he never so much as mislaid a hook-eye.

They were old and she was old, but they were older than she, and I think that the contrast between them gave her a sense of youthful power. I have seen an aged mother be almost a fountain of youth. There lives here an old woman who is upwards of ninety, and with her live her unmarried daughters, —women well along in their sixties.

The old lady still calls her daughters "the girls," and orders them about smartly. They are all of the old school and they obey her very well, but in turn they tyrannize over her, look after her; "do for her," as we have it here. One can never drop in on them without their having a story to tell about some new rash deed of "mother's"; and so they are young in spirit, having a work to do in the world; some one to run, and no chit of a younger generation to run them. Another reason for their youthfulness is that the house has not had so much as a new matchsafe for twenty years: they yet have about them things all of their own choosing; they have not had to part with the familiar friends of their youth.

My mother's house was like this.

While she was particular about repairs, new things she would not buy. With-in-doors, combined with an austere order, there was a certain dilapidation of armchairs due to over-use; the lamp was old; everything about her had been used for years, and the presents which we made her stuck out like so many sore thumbs,—I am sure that many of them disappeared into cupboards and drawers when we took our departure.

And when we broke up our larger house in which we lived, and she and father came to live in this little one, I remember she gave us with lavish hand what seemed to us the pick of the furniture, and kept for herself those things that belonged to her earlier years.

45

Have you ever noticed when it is that people have their houses "done over"? I have. It usually occurs soon after the daughters have been "out" a while, and have had time to develop a taste of their own. Then the moment comes when the furniture is rearranged, new touches are added, old-fashioned things sent away to the attic for a long rest, and the house passes from the older generation to the younger. The altered aspect of the house shows that the young people are beginning to take possession of their own. Do you remember when so many of the parlor carpets throughout the land were done away with and little slippery rugs put in their places?— and a wonder it is that we did n't all break our necks sliding across the floor on them!

46

I have an old friend who picks her way gingerly across the shining, polished floor, as much in fear for her poor stiff bones as if she were walking on ice. As she walks carefully from one treacherous oasis of a rug to another and deposits herself on a Chippendale chair, I can but remember the time when the room was full of billowy, upholstered chairs, faulty in line, perhaps, but holding out ample, inviting arms to you. And as she perches herself on the uncompromising colonial furniture, I know that she regrets her comfortable old chairs, though she bravely pretends she thinks the new furniture a great improvement.

Here is another of the milestones of age; we pretend as hard as we can that we like many things we don't like, that

47

we may not seem old-fashioned to our
dear ones. We do what we can to keep
pace with them until our old legs are
weary with running; but our children,
do the best we may, are far in advance
of us. We make concession after concession of our own preferences, even
to giving up the things that lived with
us when we were young and which
grew old with us and old-fashioned
even as we did. To please our children
we treacherously discard them, pre-
tending we think them, in their old-
fashioned comfort, as hideous as do
our young people. My friend points
out the purity of design of the new
furniture,—but she has had one of the
old parlor chairs done over and put in
her own bedroom. She sits there a good
deal. I have noticed that older women

work and read much in their own rooms, and I sometimes wonder if it is n't because the rest of the house has become strange and unhomelike.

CHAPTER III

I CAN remember when I was a young woman how many of my mother's foibles fretted me, for I was like the rest. I had n't reasoned it out any more than most people do, but I held some immutable opinions about the conduct of age. If I had my life to live over again, I should know better. I should cherish each of my mother's restless days, because I would know that her very restlessness and occasional discontent were the signs that life was keen within her, and that I myself had made her restless, because as a too zealous daughter I had in a measure, together with Time, taken from her some of the occupations

that still by right belonged to her. I
would let her have her way on all the
minor points of dress and occupation.
I would not criticize the old workmen
she chose ; and, above all, I would not
try to impose on her any of my ideas
of how an older woman should act.
For young people have hard-and-fast
notions concerning older women's actions. When we depart from them,
they make a personal grievance of it.

I do not think I am exaggerating
when I say that there is no class of
society so bound down by convention,
and for no good reason, as are the oldest of all. A young and pretty woman
must, of course, walk carefully along
life's paths; she must take care to
avoid even the appearance of evil. As
she grows older, a suitable amount of

convention in the mother of a family is a wholesome balance. But when a woman grows old, when she has climbed the ladder of years beyond the point where scandal could touch her, one would think that she might lay aside minor conventions of life; that at last she might do what she pleased, only limited by her own failing strength. There are so few things, after all, left for us to do, so few that we have the heart left for, or the wish for now, that it would seem only right that we should follow our caprice in the small matters that still belong to us.

I recently heard a young woman my daughter's age complain somewhat after this fashion: —

"There are no more real grandmothers left in the world! I don't know what the nowadays children are going to do. How much my dear old grandmother meant to me! As far back as I can remember, her sweet white head, crowned with its snow-white cap, was always at her favorite window in summer, and in winter she sat beside the open fire with her feet upon a little hassock, like Whistler's mother. We children always knew where to find grandma. She was always so glad when we came. I can see yet the welcome in her eyes when we would run in on her. She would invent little games for us and tell us little stories as long as we would stay. The lovely part of it was that she was always *there*. No matter if mother was out, or any one else, we could be sure of finding *grandma* ready to hear all about our little joys and troubles."

During this little recital, which, of course, was not a long peroration, but was given to us in the broken phrases of a conversation, I had a very vivid picture of this old lady, probably only a few years older than myself, who was " always there." What infirmity, I wondered, made her be there all the time? When an older woman is " always there," depend upon it, there is some deeper reason and a sadder one than that she was waiting for her little grandchildren. No one knows this better than I myself, for I, too, am " there," for one reason or another, more than I wish to be. Oh, I knew very well how eagerly she waited for those little grandchildren of hers, and how the lonely, gray, spacious hours brightened up in the flicker of their laughter. I knew,

too, as they got over being little babies,
how brief their sweet, tumultuous visits
must have been. It is only very little
children who spend much time in their
grandmother's skirts. For a long time
past I have been conscious that Betty
only stays with me when she is kept in
or has nothing better to do. Once a
child has grown into liberty, you may
be sure it will not spend overlong
spaces of time with its grandparents,
unless they, too, are active enough to
be in the field, like an old English
friend of mine who, at seventy-three,
with undimmed enthusiasm, is teaching
his grandchildren to ride and shoot and
whip a trout stream. You may depend
upon it that they idolize him, not because
he is "there" all the time, but because
he can do all these things better than

they can, and is, besides, a living spring of fishing-tackle, rods, and other sporting goods.

But this was not all my friend had to say. After her picture of her own poor grandmother, she took up the first part of her argument.

"Nowadays," said she, "I look around in vain for sweet old ladies like my grandmother. There do not seem to *be* any old ladies any more; they seem to have gone out of fashion along with the dear, pretty caps they used to wear, and that they looked so sweet in. Nowadays older women dress just like their daughters. Instead of ever being where their grandchildren can find them, they are off, if you please, at clubs or playing cards or even taking a jaunt in a motor-car!"

She said this, mind you, under my very nose, and I did n't know whether I was vaguely pleased with the subtle flattery that she ignored the fact that I was a very case in point of her recalcitrant new-fangled grandmother, or whether to feel a little vexed with her for being so obtuse. For a moment I entertained the idea of allowing myself the luxury of playing at being her age, and then I felt I had better come out flat-footed, and say, " Well, Eleanor, I suppose you think I had better wear a cap and give up the whist club"; but I knew she would answer, with a look of naïve wonder in her soft brown eyes, " Why, auntie, *you 're* not old !" So all I said was, " I suppose, my dear, the conditions of life are easier and the doctors are better, so nowadays many older people manage to keep their infirmities at bay a little longer."

I think that back of Eleanor's ideal of a grandmother there lay a good deal or unconscious selfishness. An elderly mother who sits contentedly by the fire all day is a far smaller responsibility than a mother that one can never put a hand on, and who, at a moment's notice, goes off on perilous expeditions.

Everything Eleanor had said about her grandmother had ruffled me more than it should, so after I got over my impatience, I asked myself why I had been so annoyed, after all. I found the answer soon enough. In lamenting that there were no grandmothers left like hers, Eleanor had clearly defined the position that the average person takes toward older women.

Each generation permits a different type of young girl, but the older woman must not change; her outline is fixed and immovable. She must be like Eleanor's grandmother, "always there," — waiting, waiting, with a smiling face through the long, quiet, empty hours, for her grandchildren to come home.

I read a clever poem the other day, the refrain of which was, "I'm looking forward to old age."

"Then," said the young writer, "at last I can be perfectly comfortable. I can lay aside the minor conventions along with my tight shoes and tight corsets. I can at last do as I please. I'm looking forward to old age."

When this young woman arrives at the Land of Old Age, though, indeed, she may, it is true, lay aside shoes that

are too small and clothes that are too
tight, she will, on the other hand, find
a whole new set of rules and regulations
to live by, and regulations that are not
self-imposed, but imposed by custom
and enforced by the younger generation. There she will find waiting for
her an ideal of what she should be herself, — the ideal which was attained by
Eleanor's poor grandmother; a grace-
ful, shadowy person, sitting, her feet
on a hassock, like Whistler's mother;
some one who has none of the impulses
of youth, which, in a grandmother, the
younger generation finds so disconcert-
ing. Even the costume of this ideal is
decided upon by our exacting young
people. She shall wear, our ideal grandmother, soft black or gray draperies, a
piece of beautiful old lace at her neck,

or a white fichu of rare old-fashioned workmanship crossed on her bosom. Caps are no longer the fashion, — but our custom-ridden children regret them.

For myself, should I live to be ninety, I hope I shall fall short of this ideal in all respects. I do not wish to become a mere ornamental nonentity about whom people shall say, "What a sweet old lady!" I hope that I shall keep my family alert over my misdeeds until my end, for then I shall be sure that I shall not have slipped altogether among the shadows before I go.

Think what the ideal of old age that seems so beautiful implies; it means that the body has so lost its resiliency that the wholesome desire for action has passed, that one's own life and actions have ceased to have an interest for one,

61

and that instead of having to snatch time to play with one's grandchildren, one has nothing to do but wait,— nothing in the world to do but "be there." It is too great a price to pay for conforming to an ideal whose greatest value, after all, lies in a certain picturesqueness. I do not think, either, that any middle-aged woman would consciously choose to have her own mother one of these ideal grandmothers, although there are ways in which each one of our daughters would be glad to have us conform to an ideal of elderly conduct a little more closely.

There are daughters who, like my own, limit the field of their mothers' activities, believing firmly that they are doing so in the interest of their mothers' health. There are a great many other middle-aged women whom I see about me who constantly curtail their mothers' personal liberties, because these old ladies wish to do things which, if you please, shock the fastidious daughters in what they think is fitting for the aged. These young women know so definitely what an older woman may and may not say and do and wear!

"Mediæval" is a word I hear often nowadays on the lips of the young people. So-and-So has "mediæval" ideas on the subject of divorce or what-not. All older people are supposed to hold "mediæval" ideas, and when it turns out that one of us happens to have read and digested a new economic theory or some new book of vital interest, it is always an irritating moment to me when a younger woman remarks, in a patronizing way, " Why, how Mrs. So-and-So keeps up with the times!" But there is no reactionary older woman I know who holds as "mediæval" opinions as those which the ordinary younger women have about the older generation. The broadest-minded women I know are as tradition-bound as possible when it comes to what we older women may do.

Many an older woman, for instance, finds a style which especially suits her, — a style which does not conform to the costume in which the poetical imagination pictures the dwellers in the Land of Old Age. I had an old friend who happened to fancy, as accessories to a costume in which to pass her declining years, a bustle and a certain false front. Bustles went their way, and a few people still clung to them;

64

then even the faithful gave them up,
but my friend still wore hers valiantly.
It suited her so to do, — and why not?
Had n't she followed the fashions long
enough? Had n't she earned her right
to wear what she chose? That was the
way she looked at it. She was a valiant,
high-spirited old lady, full of good-
tempered anecdotes about every one
you ever heard of, fond of all the
bright things of life, — young people,
dance music, company, and bright
colors; the last she wore unflinchingly.
So gayly indeed and gladly did she
walk up the road of time that she died,
advanced in years, without old age having seemingly laid a finger on her blithe
spirit. If the young people had a quiet
smile at the expense of her bustle, it
was a tender one. The false front which

she wore with great artlessness was an ornament to her personality. None who loved her, and they were many, would have had her altered in any respect. There was but one exception to this — her widowed daughter, who with her little girls made her home with her mother. The bustle and false front caused her the keenest pain. I do not believe my friend ever got herself ready for a "party" without the daughter trying to decrease the size of that bustle. She never gave up trying. I remember waiting for my friend and hearing in the hall above me the sounds of argument, and at last from the stairs my friend's voice: "For the hundredth time, Emily, I will *not* go out looking like a pancake! I tell you I should n't feel decent!"

She came into the room, her flowing
silk rustling and creaking, her bonnet
brave with colors, and I could n't, as
I looked at her, understand how any
daughter, however hide-bound, could
have wished to alter a hem's breadth of
her high-hearted, courageous costume.
My friend loved every one to be happy
and contented around her, and I often
think how many small annoyances she
might have been spared had her daughter not had such firm convictions concerning the conventional dress of age.
I am glad to relate, however, that my
old friend wore her bustle, her daughter notwithstanding, almost to her dying
day. I hope they buried it with her, —
she made a brave fight for it. She is to
me an inspiring memory. When my
children try — oh, very gently — to take

67

from me some little habit or some peculiarity of dress, I think of her and smilingly hold on to my own, for I will not encourage them in their stupid and "mediæval" idea of the fitness of things. I will not, at my time of life, have my individuality pruned and clipped. In the matter of dress there are endless limitations for us older people. All the lighter colors are supposed to be unsuitable for us; and so for some of us they are from an æsthetic point of view, though I have known many a middle-aged woman and many a pink-cheeked, snowy-haired grandmother to whom pale pink would have been every bit as becoming as the pale lavender which custom permits. .

I know one sweet old lady who has always loved pink as a favorite color.

She confessed to me that it was a cross to her when she grew too old to wear it.

"Well, why don't you anyway?" I asked her, knowing very well why. *I* would not have the courage to blossom out in so much as one daring pink ribbon, but, "Why don't you?" said I.

"I do," she replied mysteriously, "I do."

I looked at her simple black gown.

"Oh, not on the *out*side! But," said she, lowering her voice, "I always run in plenty of pink ribbon in my things, and I have pink ribbon garters!" she concluded triumphantly.

And only an older woman who has been cut off by an arbitrary custom from many of the pretty gay things of life will understand what a comfort those pink ribbon garters were to her.

69

One of my friends has already reached the age of eighty without her interest in life being in any degree abated, and, what is far rarer, without her desire to be up and doing being in any degree diminished by age's infirmities. She has, perhaps, a more transparent look than she had some fifteen years ago, but she is still as erect as a girl. Except for looks, for her beautiful white hair and her old-lady dresses, — she happens to be one who takes kindly to the wearing of lace fichus, — she is everything that conventionally an older woman should not be. You do not find her "there," —not she; and not only is she not there, but she does n't tell her daughters where she is going. They are between Margaret's age and mine, and discuss "Mother's" wild, headstrong ways in my presence. She gives them a great deal of trouble and anxiety, and it is n't all by any means simple worry for fear she may do herself some harm or over-tax her strength. She keeps a life of her own. Since her daughters have in the natural order of things assumed the helm, she has interested herself in vari-ous intellectual pursuits; she attends lectures not only here, but in the sur-rounding towns. She is valiant in the field of missionary labor. As her daugh-ter sighs: "It seems to me we never send out cards for *anything* that mother does n't take that time for getting up barrels for the Indians!" You see, her activities interfere with the family, and they will neither let her go her way unmolested nor will they accept her activity without protest. She is, and

71

partly because of these arbitrary conventionalities, a great care to her daughters.

One of them came in the other day sighing: —

"Well, I've got to go with mother to Elenwood to hear that man lecture on 'Labor Conditions' to-day. I *don't* see where I'm to find time."

"Your mother couldn't go alone, I suppose?" I asked tentatively.

"She could," replied this poor daughter, "for she's to meet friends at the other end, but it *looks* so bad for a woman of mother's age to go around the country alone. As if her children cared nothing for her!"

It would be a great relief to them all if this active old lady would stay at home more. I am glad she does n't. My

high-spirited friend is one of those who
are helping to kill out the conventions
which are troublesome weeds in the
Land of Old Age.

CHAPTER IV

ANOTHER convention that shackles the lives of most older women is the methods which their grown children employ to conserve their elders' health. Each family has its own particular fetish as to what "Mother" ought to do for her health; almost all older women who have their children living with them have to submit themselves to the hygienic fads of their sons and daughters. In my own case it is carriages; they are the bane of my life. I could keep an accurate record of how years are crowding on me by the way my children send me around instead of letting me walk. When Margaret begins, "Colds are terribly preva-

lent at this time of year. Have you
heard, Dudley, that Mrs. Sears has got
pneumonia ? " — then I know that she
wants me to drive to the reception or
wherever I am going.

To any one who has not passed from
middle age into the place where people
live who are already counted old, it
may seem a far cry between Mrs. Sears's
pneumonia and my having a carriage
on a sunny fall day, but those who are
living in that country where older people dwell will understand. To listen to
our children talk to us, you might think
that all we older people might live a
thousand years if we only did all the
tiresome, unpleasant things for our
health that our children want us to do,
and I suppose that I ought to be glad
that my Margaret has a mania for car-

75

riages. That is the word for it,—a
mania. At the slightest excuse I am
driven in a jolting, germ-laden, livery-
stable hack to and from the reception,
concert, or lecture or church. This
procedure has saved me, according to
Margaret, all the diseases and ailments
of mankind except perhaps the bubonic
plague, and if that disease were preva-
lent in our neighborhood, I dare say
Margaret would find means of proving
a carriage had saved me that.

Still, there are friends of mine whose
daughters have so much more unpleasant ways of preserving their mothers'
lives, that I should be glad that it is
nothing worse than hacks.

My friend, Mrs. Wellington, for instance, is taken out and walked and
walked about until she almost drops,

because her children believe that people get old and stiff because they don't walk enough. As if it wasn't because they are stiff in their joints that makes them want to keep quiet!

Mrs. Granger is dreadfully afraid she will have to give up breakfast, which is a meal she has always especially enjoyed, just to keep peace. Every little turn of any kind that she has, her children put down to her liking for griddle - cakes and syrup in the morning, since they have gone in for the no-breakfast fad. She says that every time she eats a good comfortable breakfast, the family sit around with faces as long as her arm, and she is just on the point of giving in, although she knows it will be bad for her.

Mothers cannot bear to see their

children worried and distressed, and it is here that we are as much at our children's mercy as we were when they were little things at our knee and could always get around us with tears welling to the eyes and quivering upper lip.

When Margaret spoke last about a carriage, she had a little worried expression on her brow that was so like Margaret when she was two years old that I would go to church in a hay-wagon to please her. I never could bear to see that little puzzled, distressed look on her face. So I submitted with fairly good grace to the proposition that I should go to Mrs. Carter's reception in the hack. I made a little protest, however, because, unless I did that, I should soon lose the use of my legs altogether and perhaps degenerate into a person who has to be pushed around in a wheel chair before I am much older. I said: —

"Well, Margaret, I will go to-day just to please you, but the next time I am going to use my own judgment about it. I have been going in a carriage all summer to avoid sunstroke and apoplexy, and now that fall has come, I must avoid pneumonia and tonsillitis, and in the winter I shall be avoiding slipping on the ice; but there's got to be some cranny in the year when I can go to places on my own two feet."

But while I will submit to carriages, I will not submit to everything, and I draw the line at a trained nurse every time I am a little ill. Recently I sent one of them flying, and while I might have made the scene easier for every one, still it did me good to get rid of that woman in the summary way I did, —or, rather, made Margaret do; for this was one of the occasions when I shirked and took advantage of one of the privileges age gives us. Indeed, I went so far as to tell Margaret that the trained nurse or I would leave the house.

Of course, when I am really ill and prostrate, and have to be watched at night, then I am willing to have all the discomforts — to say nothing of the needless expense — of having such a woman about. But when I am well, or pretty nearly well, to have a capped and aproned and uniformed woman, with a strong, dominant will, following my every footstep and bringing me unpalatable things to eat every two hours, — why then, I shall always rebel, as I have done this time.

I said to Margaret: "This illness has been a trying one to me in every respect. I have never had to keep in my bed any longer than a morning at a time since you were born. I have lain in bed now six days; three of these days I might as well have been up."

At which Margaret replied: "I am sure you are better for the rest, darling."

I know I'm not. The reason I know this is that the last three days, whenever the nurse and Margaret left me alone to go down and get some unpleasant eatable from the kitchen for me, I got up and sat in my rocker at the window, which rested my back, though I hated to hurry back to bed, as of course I had to do whenever I heard them coming. So I might just as well, as you can see for yourself, have been up and dressed all the time, without having the nervous strain of listening for their return.

Then, too, the first day I was ill, I dressed and went downstairs. Everybody made a great outcry, and they sent for the doctor again, for the sole purpose of making me do as they said. He is a very sensible young man, and I approve of a great many of his ideas, but at the same time, like most of the modern school, he carries much too far the modern theory of keeping a person in bed until his muscles grow weak and his back aches, though, of course, he is not nearly so unreasonable about this as my own children.

"I'd like to ask you a simple question, Doctor," I said to him when he told me that, as long as my temperature was above normal, I would have to stay in bed. "How do all the workingmen do — all the people with livings to earn — when their temperatures go to 102?"

He pretended, when they have a fever, that even workingmen have to stay at home first or last; but I don't believe it. When people have to earn a living, nothing will convince me that they pop thermometers down their throats every time their stomachs get upset.

What neither the doctor nor my children understand is that I know more about matters concerning my own health than any one else. During my long life I have, of course, had my ups and downs of health like other people, and with the advancing of years, especially the last three, my strength and endurance have lessened perceptibly, and I, like other middle-aged people, have had to give myself care, so I have learned pretty well what things to avoid and how to treat my own idiosyncrasies.

During this illness, how I longed for some of those old, easy-going days, when, even though I did n't feel well, I managed to get downstairs and sit quietly around with my book or even have a whiff of fresh air; and how I longed for the days when I lay down or sat up as I felt inclined, instead of lying rigid and aching in my bed, watched like a cat by a strange woman from morning till night and from night till morning. How I disliked that cot put up in my bedroom for her to sleep in!

And this was not the worst of it. It seemed to me as if that woman deliberately hid all my things. One would think, for instance, that, having made a painful attempt to do my hair, — and she almost pulled out the few remaining strands that are left me, and with which I am naturally unwilling to part, — it would have occurred to her to replace the brush and comb and other articles where she found them. When I slipped out of my bed to do my own hair in a comfortable way, I could find nothing whatever to do it with; all my toilet

85

articles, which ordinarily I could have put my hand on in the dark, had disappeared. I looked all over the room for them; they had vanished utterly as if she had swallowed them. I wandered up and down, trying to find them, and, I will confess, so vexed that I had n't any ears for Margaret's approach. When she came into the room and found me up, she exasperated me still more by saying, "Why, darling, how did you happen to be up? Why did n't you let the trained nurse get whatever you wanted?"

"Margaret," I said, "keep that woman out of here for fifteen minutes, because I don't want to say anything that I shall be sorry for later. I suppose she does what she conceives to be her duty, but a more disorderly and ill-

trained woman it hasn't been my lot to
meet. Where's my toothbrush? Where
are my brush and comb? What has she
done with my licorice tablets? And I
can tell you frankly that if she has
touched my pen and paper, — even
though I don't want them now, — I
shall have to tell her what I think of
her. Be so kind as to find my brush and
comb so that I can do my hair with
some comfort. Trained nurses ought to
be taught not to do one's hair up in
wads and make them feel like English
walnuts to lie on!"

I don't pretend that this was a gra-
cious speech, and it is not the way that
I usually feel or talk to any one, especially to my daughter. I merely quote
myself to show to what a state of exas-
peration a woman of my age and train-

87

ing may be driven. That woman was there to take care of my health; the reason I suffered her about me at all was to save my family anxiety. But it is extremely trying for a woman of my years, except in cases of the most dire necessity, to have fussing about her person an outsider who upsets all her little personal ways; meddles with her personal belongings, and renders her far more uncomfortable than comfortable. I am sure that my temperature remained above normal partly through the continual irritation that I suffered because of these things.

Then, too, I know it was not good for me to have to watch every chance to slip out of bed to brush my own teeth. Brushing my teeth in bed, or, worse still, allowing some one else to brush them for me, is a thing which I should have to be far sicker than I have ever been to have happen to me. When I give up getting out of bed to brush my teeth of my own accord, then my children may know I'm really ill, and can send, if they like, for a day nurse and a night nurse, for I shall be past caring how many troublesome and disorderly women I have about me.

Three times in one night she got up to ask me if I spoke, or if I wanted anything, just because I cleared my throat as it's my habit to do. Finally I said to her: "Miss Jenkins, if you came to my bedside less often, my chances of going to sleep would, I think, be greater, and I'm sure it is better for your health as well as mine for you to remain in your own bed."

89

All of which shows under what a nervous pressure I have been forced to live. I explained my point of view to Margaret after the departure of the nurse. I said to my daughter: "Margaret, I'm taking five kinds of pills and tonics, and as I've lived with my own stomach now a large number of years, I am perfectly sure that the reason why my appetite remains so poor is that I'm constantly dosing, and you need bring me no more of those strychnine tablets and you can put the pepsin away, and as for the liquid things in bottles, I won't take them either."

I stuck to this for quite a little while, but Margaret had got it into her head that my whole life and existence depended on a few little pasteboard boxes of pills. Lines that I don't re-

member having seen in her face since
Betty was so ill appeared there. Finally, she came to my bedside and took
my hand and said: "Mother, I simply
can't bear to see you trifling with your
health in this way, and I don't think it's
fair to us to do as you are doing. You
can't get well, and you can't get strong,
unless you will take care of yourself."

Her tone and her whole manner
touched me, and I saw what people who
live in the Land of Old Age sometimes
forget,— how great and pressing the
things we know to be of little importance
seem to our great, grown-up sons and
daughters. There was in Margaret's
tone and in her attitude almost that
poignant agony that a mother has over
her sick child.

She could not bear to have me sick.

I saw then that each meal that I could not eat, each time I did not take my medicine, — even my just rebellion against my trained nurse, — had taken from her a little of her strength and vitality.

It is hard, when one is ill and suffering one's self, to realize the extent to which this reacts on those about us, especially for us older people. I had a quick vision of Margaret's seeing me walking off wantonly, needlessly, into the land of shadows. I know, of course, that when the day comes, pills and trained nurses and gruel will not retard my footsteps, and I shall very much like to pass through the series of minor illnesses that may be before me in my own way, comfortably, without too much nagging and without having my hair-

brushes hidden, or having to lie in bed
when I know it is bad for my back. But
after all, I think I saw on that morning
that my annoyances had been small
compared to Margaret's anxieties. She
threw aside for the moment the smiling
" You-will-be-better-to-morrow " mask
that she had consistently assumed from
the beginning of my illness, and I realized for the first time that the week
had been one where shadowy fears had
pressed about her, taking from her her
gayety, her confidence. Each time I
had sprung from my bed to get something I wanted, she had seen the
shadows about me ; each moment of
my weakness had whispered desolation
to her.

I thought of the long evenings that
she and Dudley had passed together,

discussing with the trained nurse my shortcomings and my willfulnesses; and I saw that my small rebellions had been to her not small rebellions at all, but willful throwing away of so many of the days that it may be yet permitted us to pass together.

For one moment I was almost sorry that I had sent that woman away, but that moment of weakness did not stay long, because, after all, it's I who will have to be the judge of how to lengthen out the span of those days. At the same time, as we sat there together in silence, Margaret holding my hand and I looking at the anxious lines in her face, I made up my mind to take the pepsin and the strychnine and all the other things that they make such a fuss over.

So I told Margaret when she implored (and I can't translate to you her accent of anxiety), " Now do take the medicine the doctor left for you ; it certainly will strengthen you," — "I will, Margaret."

But even then a flicker of spirit rose in me ; for all of Margaret's and Dudley's agonizing, I'm not dead yet, — very far from it, — and it's very seldom that I get a good chance to influence my children's lives. So that is why I said to my daughter : —

"Margaret, I can see that you are very anxious about me. But I'm equally anxious about you, though I don't presume to nag you and make such a fuss about it. I will take the tablets and the tonics and the powders, and even the horrid things put up in gelatine capsules, which are as hard to swallow as
95

any hen's egg in its shell, if you will
make a few concessions on your part:
that heavy tailored skirt that you've
been wearing I know is the cause of
your backache. Will you promise me
to put it aside, for a while anyway?"

"Yes, mother," Margaret agreed.

" And will you try to eat your meals
more regularly?" (For Margaret has
been doing a great deal of outside club
work, and half the time comes home to
lunch ten or fifteen minutes late, when
all the meat is cold and spoiled, and I
know that it will injure her stomach in
the long run.)

"Margaret," I said, "I've studied
the rules of health for a great many
years, and as you are fond of boasting,
I'm in pretty good condition as a rule,
considering my time of life and the

things I've been through. So if I'm to do what you want me to, I think it is only fair that you should, in smaller matters, be guided by me a little bit; and this sitting and reading so far from the light and spoiling your eyes is a thing that has got to be put a stop to, if I am to take another strychnine tablet."

Margaret agreed readily to all these things. It may seem to you that I was taking an unfair advantage; but I do my share of silent worrying on my own side, and it seemed to me only fair exchange, because undoubtedly it will benefit my health to be saved these small anxieties, besides benefiting Margaret's.

Margaret agreed readily because I think she saw the reasonableness and justice of my remarks.

"May I bring you tapioca now?" she asked at the end of my talk.

"No, Margaret," I replied. "I am going down to dinner to-day, and I am going to eat some solid food-things that I *want* to eat, which I know will be much better for my health."

CHAPTER V

I GRUMBLE a good deal, it seems to me, about my children's too anxious care of me; I make life seem shorn of many of its pleasures,—and so it is; but age also clips life of complications. It is the great simplifier.

For instance, the moment my eye fell upon my new neighbors, I knew I was n't going to like them. This may sound as though I am disagreeable and ill-natured, but I don't think I am. Indeed I have lived so long in this world that I feel free to express my opinions without being afraid of being misunderstood. A younger woman might not give out so frankly what she thinks, as she

99

has her reputation to make ; but one opinion, more or less, of my neighbors, will not alter my reputation, for if I have proved myself, in the long time I have stayed in this world, kindly and not hard to please and ready to make allowances, I believe people will make allowances for me, and it will not hurt me one bit to ease my mind by saying that I do not fancy my new neighbors. I don't suppose I had any reason for it, for they seemed very nice and pleasant people.

The older woman, the one Margaret picked out as a companion for me, was fastened into one of those new-fangled frocks that have hooks in every conceivable spot where a hook ought not to be and none where they ought to be. Not that this had anything to do with

my liking her, as I have plenty of
friends of my own age who enjoy keeping up with the styles and like to have
the dressing hour one of martyrdom. I
just didn't feel that these people and I
would have anything to talk about, and
conversation would always be of that
rudimentary kind that happens on the
outskirts of acquaintance.

I said nothing about this, however,
and in a few days, when Margaret suggested we should call, "It seems," said
I, "rather damp to me to-day. You run
over, Margaret dear, so as to be nice
and cordial and leave my cards. If we
are in for a spell of bad weather, I
may not get around for a week or two."

So saying, I settled myself comfortably in my chair and told the maid to
telephone to my friend Mrs. Welling-

ton to see if she would come and play logomachy. I sat there waiting with that most comfortable of all feelings in my heart, — a feeling that comes of having decently avoided a disagreeable duty. I looked back over my long life and thought of the many times I had called and called and called on people I did n't want to, — new church people who I thought were lonely; people who were friends of friends of mine with whom I had no more in common than I had with a flagstaff.

Before she went out, Margaret asked, "Are there any more calls you don't feel like making? for I might as well do them all up, now that I am started."

At that I made out a list of all the people I did n't especially want to see in town. It was not a very large

one, for I am fond of my fellow creatures. Though, strictly speaking, my
day of calling is over, when I want to
see any one I go and see them and
spend a good hour or more in a real
talk. I am no longer a young woman;
I am an elderly woman, and will soon
be old, and the day for me, thank goodness, is past when I spend an afternoon
in that most senseless occupation, —
fifteen-minute calls, where the people
are called upon according to neighborhood, and not because any one feels any
particular need of their conversation.

In many ways, as we advance in
years, we return to the attitude we had
when we were children. If we grow
old wisely, we lay aside the senseless
forms and meaningless conventions of
society and go back to a more primi-

tive mode of social intercourse, picking our friends the way children do, — because we like them, — spending time enough with them to get some real good out of them.

It was with joy that I saw my daughter depart to call upon the Towners, for this was the name of the new people. In this world, of course Towners have to be called upon, but oh, glorious day! the time is past when it is I who must do it. If I have to forego some things I would like to do; if old age in the shape of waning strength says to me often, "Thou shalt not!" so do my years smile upon me and say to me, "Thou needst not."

I have moments of unhappiness and rebellion, as I suppose most older women have as old age creeps on them

104

unawares as they work and dream and
live; I have moments of sorrow that
my real work in the world is done, and
moments of sadness that my children
no longer come to me, but spare me,
not wishing to trouble me; but oh, with
what happiness do I leave the perform-
ing of some duties to the younger generation. Think what an emancipation it
would be if some voice should cry, —
"No more calls!" This is what the
voice of age said to me, as I sat that
afternoon by the window watching my
dear daughter ply dutifully forth. Many
years will have to pass by before she
can sit down quietly before her pleasant
open fire and rejoice that never, never
again will she need to make a duty
call.

As I watched Margaret go her way

on her round of calls, I saw all the family of tiresome duties before me; not only calls, but committee meetings of one kind and another. Not a committee meeting do I have to go to. I don't have to feel like a beggar getting money for the church organ or the new church carpet. I did these things willingly and cheerfully in my time, and now, thank goodness, I don't have to do them. I even make the confession that there are some times, when Margaret says to me, "Mother, it's too rainy for you to go to church," that I agree with her with a certain alacrity.

Oh, blessed are the immunities of age!

This morning there walked past my house a young person. She was pretty, she was young. I have no doubt that I should have been an object of pity in her eyes as I sat there in my comfortable wide chair in my comfortable dress, which, if you please, is a waist and skirt, the waist hooking in the front. This pretty young person's back hair was built out one foot behind her head with what aids I am too innocent to pretend to tell you; her frock was of the kind that fits with distressing closeness until it bursts out in a flare of pleats at the knees, and she wore upon her head a prodigious hat. Her type was not extreme. I see young women and maidens every day more fantastically and uncomfortably arrayed.

"Oh," I thought to myself, "there's a spring in youth, to be sure, and a joyousness in it, but oh, how uncomfortable youth makes itself!"

I see my daughter Margaret clawing around her spinal column, trying to hook her clothes up the back, and rejoice that I am of an age where, fashion book or no fashion book, things may yet fasten up the front. I don't need to wear a hat that looks like a chimney or a monstrous mushroom; I can wear broad, low-heeled, cloth-topped shoes while the styles in shoes skip around from heavy mannish to paper soles and pointed toes.

There are women, of course, who do not take advantage of the blessed privileges which age brings them, but, after all, not many of us. Most of us have sense given us to realize that there are certain fads in this world that we are through with.

So I confess that I saw the little girl
108

with the imposing hair and hat go her
way without envying her her youth.
Would I not like to be young again?
Who would not if they could have
youth plus the wisdom which their
years have given them?

It may be that it is "sour grapes"
that makes me feel as I do, but a pro-
found thankfulness sweeps over me
when I run through the long list of
things I need not do any more, and if
I rejoice that certain distasteful duties
are removed from me, how much more
do I rejoice over the amusements that
did not amuse me that I no longer
have to go to. No more do I have to
attend concerts of an ultra-classical
nature; no longer do I have to read
the newest book if I do not choose
to; if I am ever bored, it is not any

longer by those things which are supposed to divert me.

Fancy your life stripped of all the things that are tiresome to do, that are a weariness to your spirit. What does all this cry about the simple life mean, — this turning to nature, this camping in Maine woods, this flying to little shacks by the seashore? Not so much the desire for beauty, for that is accessible to very many people, but leisure to enjoy it, and attaining this leisure by throwing out of the window what one might call "the padding of life." I do not have to leave my comfortable home for an uncomfortable, half-furnished shanty to revel in the beauty of the maple tree which makes a golden glory outside my window. Without effort on my part life has handed me these extra

hours in which to look around the
world and enjoy the beauties of it with
peace in my heart, and it seems that for
those who look upon age rightly, life
becomes a spacious, roomy place. For
some the spaciousness means loneliness;
through the vaulted roominess of the
days voices echo infrequently; the wide
vistas of time are unpeopled and bare;
memories only walk through, — shadowy and with sad eyes. I can only
thank God that age has not come to
me in such a guise. For me and many
of my contemporaries the priceless gift
of time has been the recompense of our
having lived so long in this world; and
instead of our days being full of the
needful but distasteful duties, and clut-
tered, besides, and choked with the
pleasureless pleasurings in which I see

111

those younger than myself spending their days, we may now turn and do the things which we have always wanted to do. And for those who have lived with zest and vigor, — that is to say, those who have lived at all, — there is hardly one who has not had some pursuit or some taste which was crowded out of their lives. If you look around the world you may see any number of vigorous elderly women doing the things they wanted to do all their days, and doing them with the earnestness and relish of children at play.

CHAPTER VI

THERE are some older people to whom
life has not handed out so many vacant
spaces, and whose days yet remain
crowded, not with the unavoidable duties, but with those that others impose
upon them.

I know a valiant old lady of seventy
whose vigorous and sane presence was
of such inspiration to her many daughters that "mother" was on a perpetual
round of visits of advice and consola-
tion. As is the case with so dominant
and self-reliant a nature, she had raised
up a brood of fine women, but women
accustomed to rely upon her, even into
middle age. As happens often in such

113

cases, she first domineered over them
and they in turn ate up her time and
her leisure until she rebelled against
this tender slavery of her own creating.
One day she arose, saying, " Before another of these granddaughters of mine
gets the croup, I'm going around the
world !" — which, it seems, she had always desired to do, but had not had the
time for. So, with much dexterity, she
eluded the vigilance of her loving children, hopped upon a boat, and informed
them by telegram where she was going.

" For," she told me by letter, " I have
no intention of viewing the marvels of
this earth with a rhinitis pill popped
into my mouth by one of my daughters
every few minutes. I don't want to go
through the tombs of the Ptolemies

114

with goloshes on my feet, as I know I should have to do if one of the girls went with me."

In one's travels around the earth one meets many elderly people who, like this friend of mine, are seeing at last the sights they had planned to see all their days; fulfilling the dreams, oftentimes, of a far remote youth.

Again, it is some desire for knowledge that we indulge in in our old age. Two old friends of mine — a retired minister and his wife — are at this moment pursuing the study of biology with all the ardor of youth. Through the years of his long life this dear man and his wife had looked forward to the time when they might slake their curiosity about the wonders of the earth, and now they are doing it with the pas-

115

sion of youth. It was a real need with them and a true desire which they had always between them kept alive. I do not know any reward that a life of toil can hold more precious than this fulfill-ment of a lifelong desire.

Another friend of mine had a very full life, though she never married. She took care of her brother's house, —a complicated establishment full of guests; but always she cherished a love for the Romance languages and read much of their literature in translation; and when she had time, which was after her sixty-fifth birthday, she learned Spanish and French and Italian.

At this minute, down the street Mrs. Baker is making rugs and carpets out of all the rags she has saved for the last thirty years. The story of how she has conserved these pieces is an epic, a tribute to the force and persistence of the human will. Her children, one and all, have tried to make her throw away "all that rubbish." They have pointed out to her that her collection of old pieces was a mania, and that nothing would ever come of it; also, they might be doing "somebody some good." During her absence her daughters would lead commiserating friends to the attic and show them rag-bags bursting, trunks overflowing, bureau drawers yawning, with the pieces their mother had collected. Oh, the younger and older generations had some doughty passages-at-arms over what the younger women called a "needless and unhygienic accumulation."

"Some day," Mrs. Baker persisted,

"I intend to make rag carpets from them — when I have time."

She has time now, and, I am glad to say, is doing what she always wanted to. The making of rag carpets may not have been a high goal to aim at, but what matter? The longer I live, the more I believe it is the spirit in which we do things that makes our acts pleasing or displeasing to a Greater Intelligence. Who knows whether rag carpets made with a cheerfulness which is in itself a prayer may not be more pleasing to the Lord than much more pretentious occupations performed sadly?

To many of us the moment of leisure comes too late; we allow the daily occupations of our business to crowd upon us so in middle life that, when old age comes upon us, it finds us without re-

source. So it is with men, while women
fill up the depths of the spirit with a
countless reiteration of detail, bank-
rupting themselves; leaving themselves
dependent upon the good will of others
for all amusement.

Many of us have worked so hard and
life has treated us so ungently that all
the fair lights that burned for us in the
country of youth have been put out;
but, thank God! it is n't so with all.
That elusive moment, "when I have
time," that every one talks about, comes
to almost all of us, and it finds a certain
number of us with a will to do what we
like. But here with the things that we
want to do, we often find ourselves in
the position of children who plan out
tasks that their little strength will not
perform. For ever and ever we bruise

119

ourselves against the limitations of the flesh. Oh, the books that we wish to read, for which our eyes do not serve; the pleasurings denied us; the work cut away from us because of the limitation of our strength, and the knowledge that this limitation must always increase. The size of the earth over which one may roam shrinks day by day, until it decreases to the house, — to one's room, — to one's bed; and finally to the narrowest space of all.

So side by side with the things that we can now do because we have more time are the things that we have no strength for and the things that our children promise to do for us and never get around to, — our children who are so eager to perform all sorts of small kindnesses.

I know that I have been wanting for three years to straighten my attic the way I would like to see it done, and neither have I been permitted to do it, nor will my children do it for me. It is one of those things that has got to be done by one of the family; no cleaning-woman can do anything except the heavier part of the work. And now, whenever I go up and sort over a trunk of letters or a chest of drawers, some one is sure to hear me walking around up there and come after me, until what Margaret and Dudley call my "attic face" is a joke in the family. They pretend that there is a certain joyful but furtive look comes over me when I have "designs," as Dudley says, on the attic.

"That attic, I hope, will never get

cleared," he tells me. "It is all the joy
to you that a double life would be. It
gives you the joy of forbidden fruit. As
long as it is n't cleared, you can sneak
up there and go on a terrible debauch;
of course you are generally ill and miserable after it, but who minds that when
they have made a night of it?"

In this disrespectful way does my son
joke me, not realizing that the state of
the attic is a real source of annoyance
to me.

Almost every older woman has something equivalent to my attic. Oftentimes
this attic is a thing a woman is strong
enough to do herself, but which her
children, with their too loving care, pre-
vent her doing. Sometimes little household duties that she has attended to all
her life herself, from one day to another,

122

her children have decided she is n't strong enough to do. Perhaps one time she got tired ; who does n't ? Young people as well as old get tired. And sometimes I think that those old people are most to be envied, after all, who keep forever in the harness and to whom each day brings its compulsory duties ; in them lies the essence of youth, which, after all, I suppose, has a good deal to do with the feeling that one is helping to make the wheels of the world's work go round.

I think that many a woman has had her life shortened by this fretting that might have been avoided, much more than it would have been by the fatigue that doing what she wished to would incur. When day after day one asks those young people, upon whom one

123

has become dependent for some service, to look after this or that, the chains of age weigh heavily. We have to ask in all the varying tones that the dependent must use, from the cajolery with which we get our own way to the futile bursts of irritation, and in the end perhaps resort to subconscious strategy, lucky at last if we can but accomplish our purpose. When I do this there is a feeling deep in my heart of how round-about, how circuitous, are my acts, how unlike the " I " that once brought about the small things in the world that I wished to; so short a time ago I could accomplish in my life, in the ordering of my household, what I wished.

The spaces in our lives that our children have helped to empty by making it difficult for us to do those things which they consider harmful for our well-being, they try to fill up with their kindly and blundering hands. Every older woman who lives much with her children knows what I mean.

Margaret and Dudley, I know, feel that I don't see enough of women of my own age. Mrs. Allen, at the other end of the town, and I have a very good time together whenever we meet, and yet it is quite a distance — for although it is a little town where we live, it is sprawled all along the Common — for us on our old legs to run in and out, and we have managed to live half a lifetime without ever becoming intimate, notwithstanding a very real enjoyment we have in each other's society.

This liking Dudley tries to further as though it was a hothouse plant.

125

"You look 'down,' mother; shan't I telephone to Mrs. Allen? Or let me run down in the motor and get her for you." Or, "I'm just going over to Lembury; shan't I drop you at Mrs. Allen's for a half-hour?" until Mrs. Allen has become to me the symbol of "amusing mother."

When I see them at it, it touches me in my heart and it touches me in my temper as well. I don't want to be amused; I don't want to have occupation found for me. If I have nothing better to do than to sit with my hands folded, then I prefer to sit; nor does conversation like this affect me in the slightest.

Margaret will say to Dudley: —

"I think that Mrs. So-and-So has changed very much this last year. She has allowed herself to lose interest in things."

"Yes," Dudley will reply, "I think an older woman makes a great mistake not to cultivate her own hobbies."

"And beside that," Margaret will add, "keep abreast with the times. Now there is Mrs. Griscom," she went on in reproving tones, "I see her out motoring with her son almost every day."

Now here I knew what they were getting to; they wanted me to go out in Dudley's new motor. Now, if there's anything I dislike it is nasty, smelly, jouncing, child-grazing, dog-smashing, chicken-routing motors. I ride along with my heart in my mouth, — not for my own life and limbs, although those are uncomfortable enough being jounced along like a piece of corn in a

127

popper, which seems to me no way for a woman to spend her few remaining years of life; but it is for the people along the wayside whom we almost crush, — the trembling horses, the squawking hens, the frightened children that rack my nerves.

I don't like motors any more than I like trolley cars, although I ride in the cars when I have to go from one town to another, but I don't enjoy them any more than I enjoy trains. If all my neighbors want to do it and enjoy it, let them, — I don't intend to! But Margaret always had a mania for having me ride; before Dudley got the car, it was carriages, but now, under one pretext or another, they try to get me to go motoring with Dudley. They say that if I once get into the car I will get to like

it, but I know that I shall not. I shall
not get to like it any more than I shall
ever have Mrs. Allen for my bosom
friend.

These things can't be forced upon
one; we will for ever and ever, young
or old, choose our amusement from
some hidden spring within ourselves,
and if new doors are to be opened to
us of enjoyment, it is our hands that
must lift the latch, though we follow
in the lead of some beloved person.

CHAPTER VII

THE LAND OF OLD AGE

I HAVE talked, I suppose, rather fancifully about what I have chosen to call the Land of Old Age. It is because old age has seemed to me often not only a state of mind, or a physical condition, but a sort of different dimension, — an actual country where we who are older must live. Often I see people approaching its boundaries, withdrawing from them, ignoring them, and next I know, I come across a new citizen. It is an invisible country, — this Land of Old Age, — and however young you are, you have been near it. I should count you unfortunate, indeed, if in the heat of the day you had not turned into its

130

shady by-paths and lingered a moment
with its quiet dwellers. It is a very
peaceful land; there is not much work
to be done; duty is rarely seen; so seldom, in fact, that sometimes those of us
who have gone there to live for good
feel that we have passed our time of
usefulness, and have moments of hot
resentment that we are not out in the
world doing its work for it.

I feel that way myself often, and at
such times make excursions outside;
always the gentle hands of my children
lead me back to my own country. And
I sometimes feel that the reason we re-
sist taking up our places there is this
sense that we are not allowed to come
out when we wish; that we are kept
prisoners, not through our own weak-
nesses, but because there are certain

131

conventions as to what is suitable or unsuitable for us old people.

But lately I have come to believe that the people who live in the Land of Old Age have their own appointed part to play, and that they help make up the sum of life.

After all, one need not dust and sweep and make pies and cake, to be of service to those we love. We would not wish to see our little children fetch and carry, and yet they are the dearest things in the world to us. So we older people, I believe, do more than we know for those we love when we sit in our own quiet country, as I found out a little while ago when I started to make an excursion into the world that works.

The mistake our younger people make is in regarding age as a fixed

quantity. They act on the firm conviction that you are older every day you
live, whereas age is as relative and variable as youth. You have only to warm
the blood with any emotion, — joy or
relief from suspense or patriotism or
pity, — and the Land of Old Age van-
ishes; especially when there is a great
calamity, the old people troop forth as
eager to lend a hand, as strong to do
a day's work, as ever they were; and I
think it is not their fault that they so
often turn their disappointed faces back
to their familiar country without having
taken part in what is going on.

When I heard, for instance, that a
little town which squats dirty and hard-
working on the outskirts of our village
had been flooded in the spring freshet,
and that there were twenty homeless

133

families and a hundred and fifty people out of work, I was eager to help. Our whole town at once bestirred itself to do something, and I was glad that the Committee of Ways and Means met at our house, even if their ways of doing things seemed cumbrous to me. In my day when we gave benefits, we had no committees nor chairmen nor any other kind of machinery. One of the ladies went around with a notebook from house to house and asked what might be expected from each one, and her paper at the end of the day read: "Mrs. Smith, four dozen biscuits; Mrs. Jones, two layer-cakes," etc. Mrs. Jeremiah Curtis and Mrs. Henry Lessey always did the scalloped oysters. (How I should enjoy a plate of scalloped oysters like that for my supper to-night!) And in this easy fashion we brought the thing about.

But I was eager, just the same, to join the ladies assembled in my parlors. And now an odd thing happened. I suppose as one gets along in years one gets acquainted less readily with the new people; for here in my own village where I have lived over thirty years, and in my own house, I found myself an outsider, surrounded by people whom I barely knew by sight. They began the meeting in the stiff, formal way I believe is known as parliamentary, but after a little while they limbered up and began discussing the affair more naturally, and I became interested. It came over me that something ought to be done right away for these poor creatures. So I said: —

"Ladies, this party five days off is n't going to clothe those blessed children, or their fathers or mothers, for that matter, who were driven out of their homes in the night with only what they had on them."

"Why, what a good idea!" exclaimed one of the ladies.

Perhaps I am supersensitive, but it seemed to me she was surprised that I at my age was capable of any ideas at all. I was about to say that I would have a canopy-top called from the stable and make a house-to-house canvass and have a big lot of things ready to send out by the evening trolley, when some one said: "I move that we appoint an Immediate Relief Committee. Can't some one ring up Susan Millsborough? She 's just the one to push that through."

In spite of myself I felt a little disappointed, for it is a great satisfaction to do things for people one's self and to do them in *one's own way*. Before I spoke I had seen myself on the rounds in the canopy-top, but now I suddenly felt very much out of it again. Not only were there faces and methods of work new to me, but my own little idea was picked away from me and gobbled into their cumbrous modern machinery. There was a great deal of telephoning back and forth, and it was on my tongue a half-dozen times to offer to go; but I realized that the canopy-top and I, from whatever point of view one chose to look at us, were not a committee.

So I held my tongue—until I got interested again. It was to be, I gathered, a huge entertainment, with all

137

sorts of elaborations. All the simple affairs, such as we would in former times have given for two years rolled into one, would n't have made such a great affair. I who knew the slender resources of our little town so well, for we are not a rich village, found myself saying, —

"Won't the cost of getting it up take away the greater part of the profits?"

"It will be such an advertisement of the whole disaster," one of them assured me. "The other towns in the neighborhood, after our example, will feel they have to do something handsome."

There was not the least suggestion of patronage in her tone, and it was not due to her that I felt that my little remark had flown so wide of the point,

but only that we talked across the gap
Time had made between us, she on the
one side understanding the new methods, and I understanding only those I
was used to. But all the same, that
afternoon I stood on my own little ter-
ritory and listened to how people did
things in the world, with an ever-grow-
ing sense of isolation. Many of the
things in this world that are hard to
bear are no one's fault at all; they are
so because the world is as it is.

All the next day my daughter Margaret bounced in and out unceasingly.
I tried to catch her a dozen times, for
I wanted so very much to do my something, however little, for the distressed
people, — I have always been so used
to doing my share in the world. At last
I buttonholed Margaret.

"Listen, Margaret," I began.

"Excuse me for a moment, darling; there's the telephone."

After a hurried conference, Margaret pinned on her hat. I followed her up.

"Before you go," I hastened to say, "let me ask you one thing."

"I've only four minutes to catch the four-thirty-two trolley," she answered, and kissed me affectionately and dashed away.

One of the children ran after her, calling, —

"Mamma, may I — "

"Ask your uncle," called my daughter; and her tone and gesture, as though she couldn't stand one more thing, made me see under what pressure she was working.

At that moment my son Dudley

walked up the path. I was planted on the steps where Margaret had left me when she whirled by.

"Anything I can do?" he asked.

He was hurried, too, but of all my children he is the one who always has time for me.

" All I want to know is, *do* they want me to make cake for them," I said, with some spirit, for I was tired of being put off like an importunate child. I make an excellent Hartford election-cake, and it is much better on the second or third day. My cake, indeed, is famous among my children and grandchildren, and I thought that in this way I could give my mite to the poor distressed people.

" That would be awfully nice, mo-ther." Dudley's tone was apologetic.

141

"But they've already arranged for the cake, — the baker gives the material at wholesale prices and does the work. We wanted to pay for his time, but he says it will be a good advertisement. Not that yours wouldn't be lots better — "

"I wanted to do something for them," I said forlornly.

"Why, didn't you do enough? You know you've given more to the Immediate Relief Committee than you can afford. Isn't that enough?" He took my arm. "Here," he said, "let me bring your chair into the shade. It's so pleasant here this afternoon. I only wish I had the time — " and Dudley was off too.

The last thing I wanted was to sit quietly in the shade, for I am what the people around here call "a mighty spry old lady." Just how old I will not tell, for it was a convention of my generation that a woman ought not to be a minute older than she could help. I am not old enough yet, at any rate, to have taken to boasting about the remarkable number of years I have stayed in the world. But I am old enough for my middle-aged sons and daughters to boast for me about how active I am for my years, — and they boast about it as if the fair health I enjoy was some virtue of their own. Perhaps the good care they take of me *is* the reason for my being so well, but down in the bottom of my heart is the conviction that, had I followed all their advice, and led the packed-in-cotton-wool existence they have marked out for me, and sent

for the doctor as often as they have
wanted me to, I should be a bedridden
old hypochondriac at this moment instead of being so ready and willing to
do my share of work.

I sat down obediently, however, and
picked up a magazine that was lying
near by; and under pretense of reading
I reviewed the last two days, quite dis-
passionately and soberly. I had come
forth from the quiet Land of Old Age.
For a moment, in the stress of interest
for those poor homeless people, I had
forgotten that Margaret and her Committee of Ways and Means and I were
not contemporaries. I had had suggestions to give, and I had been ready and
strong to lend a hand where a hand was
needed. I had forgotten, I say, that I
am what people call "old," and now as

144

I sat idle in the shade I remembered,
and all at once I felt rather tired and
strangely aloof from the things that
were going on around me.

Through no one's fault except my
own I had been thwarted and my own
ideas taken from me. My fault was the
irreparable one of belonging to the
generation of those whose business it
is to sit comfortable in the shade and
wait — who can say for what? Just
then my little grandchild Edith came
up to me, and, without asking, took my
magazine from my hand to look at the
pictures, and it occurred to me that those
older children who had taken my work
from me — without asking, either —
had done it as serenely unconscious
as Edith was that I might want the
work for myself.

And was n't I a still older child myself ? Need I sit and sulk because the
other children would n't let me play at
their game ? They could play it better
without me, they did n't need me,
thought I, with the best philosophy in
the world, — and all the time I wanted
to be playing with them, for in my play
I would forget for a little while that I
was n't, after all, their age. I think that
our dear children who look after us so
well and see that we don't tire ourselves, and scold us gently when we
sit in drafts, — we " spry old ladies,"
— forget, in the care of our ailing
bodies, that it is better sometimes for
the body to be tired, if the spirit is n't.
It is good for us to take what part we
may in the affairs of life. The Land of
Old Age is n't, as our children think,

just a place for people to coddle themselves in. When I got so far in my thought, two more of my grandchildren ran up to me. They had been sent home from the town hall. It seems they had been in the way.

"Well," thought I, "here we are, too old and too young. We can play together if neither of us can play with the big children."

It came over me that perhaps it was just as well that we were n't all of us hurrying and working, and that at the day's end there should be some one not too tired. Just then there turned in at the gate a friend of mine. Though she is still in her twenties, she and I are the best of friends. Her pleasant face was lined with care, and she looked worried and tired.

"Dear child, what is the matter?"
I asked.

"It's that the Daughters of the
American Revolution and the Woman's
Village Improvement Society each want
to decorate the hall, and they're quar-
reling, and nothing's getting done,"
she said, and burst into tears.

I patted her head and wiped her tears
off, and we made some iced tea, and I
sent her off at last quite cheered up.

"I had to come down and get out of
it for a minute. It was so nice of you
to be sitting there so cool and rested,"
she added enviously.

Then one by one my tired, over-
worked children came home to me.
Without knowing what they did, they
turned to me for comfort and for rest,
and I took care of them and smoothed

out their difficulties, and laughed with
them and sympathized with them. They
seemed very young to me, my big children, and I realized that they turned to
me as they always had, and that I still
had things to give them and things to
do for them. What if my body must be
quiet? It seemed to me that night that
I gave them their supper and put them
to bed as I had done so many times
when they were small, for there are
blessed moments in all mothers' lives
when their grown children seem again
little children. They had come to me in
the quiet land I live in to be rested, as
every one in the world turns to that
land of peace, as all busy, hurried work-
ers and tired mothers turn into these
still, quiet roads.

There we sit, we older men and women, waiting for our children to come to us. They find us there ready to tell them how little their little troubles mean, for in our country the perspectives are long, and we look down long vistas on the road of years. In their great troubles we can say, "I know, I understand," for we have worked and have seen all the things our children must see. And if now and then the world of work calls to us, and if for a moment we like to pretend that the details of the hour are important, let us go out at will, and play at work, for in our hearts we know that we live in the Land of Old Age.

CHAPTER VIII

GRANDMOTHERS AND GRANDCHILDREN

THE human beings that are closest to
the Land of Old Age are the children.
In so many ways their limitations are
ours. Margaret has to apply the same
"Thou shalt nots" to Betty that she
does to me. For instance, I had planned
to go over for a game of backgammon
with an old friend of mine, Eliza Storrs,
and had n't paid much attention to the
weather; neither had my little grand-
daughter Betty; so each of us was
making her preparations briskly when
Margaret nipped us both in the bud.
Betty was easy enough to nip. All
Margaret had to do with her was to tell
her quite openly and frankly that to-

151

day was a nasty day, quite unsuitable for a little girl to be abroad in. It was a different story with me. I was a child of a larger growth, headstrong, and hard to manage, so my daughter approached me with tact, as one must children of my sort. She opened fire craftily in this wise : —

"Wasn't it awful about poor Mrs. Allen's hip?" said she. "I hear she isn't getting on at all." (Mrs. Allen fell the other day on a slippery pavement and broke her hip.) "Her daughter begged and begged her to take a carriage, but she wouldn't," my guileful daughter continued. "Imagine her feelings when her mother was brought home. They say she will always have to walk with a crutch."

Now a great many more people of

Margaret's age get hurt every year than women of mine, but I did n't feel like arguing the point.

"It was just such a day. I suppose it 's silly of me, but every time you go out in bad weather since then—" says Margaret, coming to the point.

"Is it bad underfoot?" I asked.

"*Awful!*" Margaret replied fervently. "People fairly skate along."

"I won't go, then," I decided.

I must say that while I see through Margaret's guile, I like to be given the semblance of choice, and so I suppose does the child who is hard to manage.

I heard Betty asking if she could n't have some little girls to play with her, and Margaret answer that she doubted if other mothers would let their children out, so I called Betty up to me.

153

In ten minutes we had both forgotten
the weather and everything else; we
might have been the same age, so much
we enjoyed each other's society.

The front door slammed, and out
·popped Margaret into the leg-breaking
weather.

"She won't let us go out, but she
goes out herself, I notice," observed
Betty, with pessimism.

I did notice, and I noticed what Betty
did n't, that she and I were housebound
for exactly the same reasons, — since
neither of us had seemed to have judgment to stay in of her own accord, Margaret, being anxious about our health,
had kept us in.

Nor was this the only place that
Betty and I met on common ground;
each one of us was dependent, each

one of us a source of anxiety to those nearest us, each one of us ministered to with the same touching devotion. Like Betty, I had my moments of rebellion, and my efforts for liberty were as futile as hers,— more futile, indeed, for each year that passed brought with it new reasons for the reasonableness of my children's tender tyranny. I suppose it is because we are so alike that the sympathy between old people and little children is as old as the world. As I sat telling stories to Betty, I could but think how, all the world over, there were grandparents rejoicing in their grandchildren, tending them, playing with them, teaching them the old baby games that go back to the beginning of time. Very often I echo in different words some observation of Betty's, — the ig-

155

norance of childhood and the wisdom
of age touch each other at more points
than one. Many of the occupations and
preoccupations of "grown people" like
Margaret seem equally profitless to
Betty and to me. We are both so far
away from the rush of events that the
passions and ambitions of the world
trouble neither of us. I have forgotten
about them, and Betty has n't found
them out, — we are on an equal footing
of indifference. Even the faults of the
grandparents and grandchildren are
alike; some of us are as self-centred
as children, and others of us have the
same naïve egotism.

There is a certain exquisite flattery
in our grandchildren's company. Betty
loves everything I do. I seem to her
witty, accomplished, and gifted. More

than this, she treats me as an equal. She is ignorant of drafts; she is not afraid all the time that I am going to tire myself out. In a word, she does n't know that when she comes to see me she comes into the Land of Old Age. She does n't know that it's because I am old that I have all the time there is, while her mother has to "make time" for her. For all Betty does for me I try to repay her by indulgences of all sorts, — sometimes by forbidden indulgences. For these I get mildly scolded, but I keep right on. I have yet to hear of a boy who grew up a bad man because of the little indulgences his grandfather showered on him, nor of one who grew up a dyspeptic because of the surreptitious cookies his grandmother gave him. I am sure I am no worse

157

a woman because my grandmother
begged me off from some well-merited
punishments. So I spoil my grandchildren as much as I can, which is as
much as I am let.

. There was a time when I wasn't allowed to spoil them at all. I hardly
knew my older grandchildren as babies,
for I went through, like so many other
women of my generation, what I call
"The Grandmother's Tragedy."

. I first heard about it from Eliza
Storrs. How often of late years I have
had occasion to think of the morning
she plumped herself down in my rock-
ing-chair. I can remember just how the
corners of her pleasant mouth were
drawn down, and in what a discour-
aged way she flapped her fan back and
forth.

"It's awfully hard work learning how to be a grandmother," she complained.

"Well," thought I complacently, "if there's one thing I shan't have to learn, it's *that*. People may have to learn how to be mothers, but not how to be grandmothers."

I was very sure of my ground because I had just that minute, you might say, got to be a grandmother myself; my arms were aching for my little grandson, whom I had never seen, my oldest son's first child. I was so full of the grandmother feeling, so eager for sight of the blessed little fellow, that I could n't believe the woman of my age existed who was n't a ready-made, accomplished grandmother.

"It's easy enough to be the kind

of grandmother *you* think you ought to, but what's hard is to be the kind of grandmother *they* want you to be," Eliza explained, flapping her fan mournfully.

I hadn't the least idea then what Eliza was talking about, so I wasn't a bit sympathetic. I wanted, indeed, to laugh, she looked so much like a fat, elderly baby herself.

At that moment a neat nurse in a cap passed the house pushing a perambulator briskly before her.

"There she is! That's the nurse!" Eliza exclaimed. "They call her a trained hospital nurse. She gets twenty-five dollars a month *and* her washing done, and if I'd had as big a family as Solomon I couldn't begin to pretend to know one half as much about babies as that woman thinks she does who's never had so much as half a one! If I had my way, oh, how quickly I'd send her flying!"

It was my first glimpse of a condition of affairs I did n't know existed.

Eliza rose to go, and sent back to me over her shoulder, —

"Mark my words, that baby's head will be flat as a pancake if they don't take her up more!"

I understood everything Eliza said soon enough. In a few weeks Ellery and Jane, the baby *and* the nurse, came home for a visit. That was when I learned first-hand about "The Grandmother's Tragedy." I think all grandmothers will agree that there is a certain emotion at the sight of your first grandchild that is a little different from

161

any other. Your son who was *your* baby
only yesterday has a little son of his
own.

I felt as other grandmothers do,—
that it was a pretty heavy responsibility
for my son and that inexperienced little
thing, his wife, to undertake, and I
guessed that they probably were as gay
and light-hearted about it as I was myself before my own children showed me
what a grave thing it was to be a mother.

"Never mind," thought I, "*I'm* here,
fortunately enough for them!" I was
ready to pour out on them the treasures
of my own experience. But more than
my desire to help them, stronger than
any wish I have known for years, was
my longing to hold in my arms my
blessed grandbaby,—it was so long

since I had held a baby of my very own. Yet, at the same time, it seemed almost a joke that I really was old enough, so soon, to have grandchildren. I thought in my ignorance that being a grandmother meant all the pleasure of having children and none of the care. So I planned and dreamed. Then came the reality and with it " The Grandmother's Tragedy."

I found out, as Eliza Storrs found out, and as so many women of my generation have found out, that I was n't to have anything, — neither pleasure nor responsibility. My empty, expectant arms were to remain empty. Jane's idea and the nurse's idea of a grandmother were negative; indeed, a grandmother was something to be guarded against. There was no room for a

163

grandmother in the routine of Roger's little life. So I remained an outsider, a spectator, and a spectator who was watched to see that she did n't make herself intrusive,— did n't, with her importunate affection, make an inroad on the rules laid down for the baby.

I 'm afraid I took it a little hard. It was such a disappointing way of setting out on one's career of grandparent, so different from that I had looked forward to with such eagerness. There is something so heartbreaking in feeling full of love, and then having your affection set aside gently but definitely as something nobody wanted. Besides that, I worried about the baby. How many times during those three weeks I echoed Eliza Storrs, — "Mark my words, that child's head will be as flat

164

as a pancake." I longed to take him up,
but actually did n't dare, though he was
my own grandchild! While Jane was
perfectly polite about it, she was as nervous as any old hen when I was near the
baby. The reason she gave for leaving
him on his back hours at a time was that
it made a child nervous to be disturbed,
and that a child, anyway, was not a
plaything.

"Perhaps," Ellery suggested once,
"he likes to be played with."

"We should n't consider what a child
likes," Jane remonstrated, and I was
sure she was quoting from a medical
book. "We should only think what is
for his good!"

So, though Roger would crow at me
in the most beguiling way, Jane or the
nurse was always on hand to see that

we never had a word in private together.

It *was* hard work learning to be that kind of a grandmother ; to my way of thinking it was being no grandmother at all. But the time came when I proved my right to love Roger in my own way. The nurse was off for an afternoon, and the baby began to cry. At first a little whimper, then a good loud roar. From the first moment it was evident to me he had an attack of colic. Jane did n't go to him at once, but continued to sew calmly. Presently she moved him over on his side and gave him a little *cold* water, but he kept on yelling, of course. Jane got up and walked the floor. Then, before my very eyes, she got down a book about babies, and read in it what to do ; I would n't have be-

lieved it if I had n't seen it for myself.
She did n't find the right place, or else
she could n't put her mind on it, for at
last she wailed out: —

"Oh, what do you think is the matter?
Oh, what do you think I ought to do?"

"I think you had better take him up,
Jane," I said gently. I was very sorry
for Jane; her outside shell of assurance
and know - it - all was, after all, only a
mask behind which a poor, inexperienced little mother lurked trembling.
"Take him up and lay him on his
stomach over a hot-water bottle. He's
got a little attack of colic."

"Thank God!" said Jane. "I thought
he might be going to have a convul-
sion!"

She was pale as a sheet, so I did it for
her. I whisked him up, and comforted

167

him just as if it had been only yesterday I had had my babies to look after. Jane watched me respectfully. She
always lifted Roger warily as if she
were afraid he would break. After that,
discipline was relaxed. I had come into
my own.

Hard as I thought my first experience was, I have learned since that it is
nothing to the humiliation some grandmothers have undergone. I have heard
of some who have been treated as if
they were contagious diseases, and by
their own daughters! I hope there are
not many such; it is too sad a way of
being cheated out of one's birthright.
There would be fewer young mothers,
I think, who mistook colic for convul-
sions, and looked up in books what it
was their babies were crying about, if

the younger generation had n't such a contempt for our old-fashioned ways. Germs are at the bottom of that contempt, though young mothers are learning daily that there is more to being a mother than in having the bottles well sterilized.

I for one protest against the " Thou shalt nots" that are written down for grandmothers. They will, of course, pass the way of many of the other useless " Thou shalt nots." But what good will that do my generation ? We shall have been defrauded of some of our rights as grandmothers, and our grandchildren will have been defrauded with us. There are some things I hold to be the right of all children from the very moment they are born, and one is the right of being spoiled by their grandparents; hand in hand with that goes the right of a grandmother to spoil them.

Age lops off our interest in one thing, then another. Year by year absence and death thin the number of our friends. Be our children never so devoted and loving, there always have been and there always will be days that have long arid places in them for people who have traveled far in the Land of Old Age. It is no one's fault. It is a part of life, no more to be complained of than the loss of the suppleness of youth. The Land of Old Age has sparsely peopled districts. Shadows move about under the shade of trees; they are the shadows of the people we used to love. Sometimes as we sit dozing in its tranquillity we hear sounds of footsteps that make our hearts beat ; the sound of dear voices comes to us, and then we wake up; they are only the dear echoes from the past, the reflections of the things that were. We know that never this side of the Great Silence shall we hear them with our waking ears.

Then to us, sitting lonely and silent, come the voices of little children ; living children, and not shadows that vanish if we dare to look at them full in the face. They are our children's children, and all at once the silent country wakes up to life. We know now why the Land of Old Age is so still and empty. It is so that the children may find plenty of room there to play. To me, in all the Land of Old Age there is no dearer sight than those old people you see with little children around them. Sometimes

it is an old man taking his little grand-
daughter out to feed the hens, or again
an old woman sitting happily, a little
sleeping child in her arms. Do not disturb her, for she had gone back years
and years, back to her own youth, and
she is dreaming that she has her own
baby in her arms.

. In the Land of Old Age how many
songs are sung every day to little children by lips that had forgotten how to
sing, for, oh, so many years! There
comes trooping to you a gay little pro-
cession of stories and games ; they
stand around you clamoring to be told
and sung and played for your grandchildren. They talk about children being
spoiled nowadays,— what with mechan-
ical toys and all ; I am sure that it is
in the homes where there are no grand-

mothers to cut paper dolls or teach how to make reins on a spool-and-pin knitting-machine. My little grandsons push spools around the room, playing they are automobiles, instead of *chu-chu* cars. Only last week I was called upon to make equipment for so recent a thing as the Spanish War. My boys fought the British, but I made the paper hats of just the same pattern for both generations ; the swords which I forged were of two pieces of wood craftily tied together by string. My grandfather taught me how when I was a little girl.

One day soon after I had won my right to be a grandmother, I was sitting with Roger in my lap, singing him one of the baby things one croons without knowing what it is.

All at once I began to listen to my-

173

self sing, with a certain surprise, as if to some one else, and these were the foolish words I sang : —

> "The craw and the poosie-o!
> The craw and the poosie-o!
> The muckle cat got up an graat
> On the top of Grannie's hoosie-o."

I had n't thought of it for years, not since I sang it to my own babies. My mother had sung it to me, and her mother to her, because back, who knows how long ago, we had a Scottish grandmother. Now all the memory of her that there is, is this old nursery rhyme, which has survived mysteriously through the changing generations. I smiled with a certain triumph to think that the women of our family would sing "The craw and the poosie-o" to their babies when all Jane's "Thou shalt nots" had been forgotten.

CHAPTER IX

YOUNG PEOPLE AND OLD

THE mothers of the little children do well to let them stay with their grandparents while they will, for soon enough they grow up.

There are always the ghosts of little children near older people, which teach them to understand the hearts of those other little children whom they meet in the real world. The grown-up children are so much harder to understand. They fill me with such a sense of ignorance, for they know so many things which I once knew and have forgotten. Indeed, almost the whole tissue of their lives is made up of these things.

I do not know why I remember my

girlhood so little, but I find that I am not alone in this. When I pin down my contemporaries, they have the same lapses of memory that I have myself. Perhaps it is because the serious things of life overshadow this time; marriage and children follow so closely on the heels of girlhood; one discovers so soon that so many of the things one has learned and almost all one has thought and dreamed have no place in the real world. So little, indeed, do I remember of this part of my life that I sometimes feel as if I had been married ever since I was a child in short dresses.

I find as I turn over the pages of the past — and so many of them are obliterated or contain only stray sentences of unrelated stories — that I can remember more about the way I felt when I was a very little girl than when I was a big one. Of the things that happened when I was at the young-lady age I remember so little: a dress, a party, a few faces, a confession of some fault that I was afraid to make to my mother. And when I finally came to her, after losing sleep, she took what I had to tell her — and I don't remember what it was — in a very disappointing, common-place way.

"Well, well," said she, "I suppose every girl is bound to make a fool of herself first or last, and I ought n't to expect you 'll escape, my dear. Let 's not discuss it further!"

I think my mother prolonged her life by refusing to discuss unpleasant things further.

Lately I have often run through these especial pages of my life, because it is only recently that I have realized what a gulf separates us older people from the younger ones. Perhaps all older women do not feel as I do, or perhaps they do not think about it at all, and imagine contentedly, as I did before Gertrude came on a visit, that because they love young people they know all about them.

Gertrude is my great-niece; she is spending her Easter vacation with us, and she is a sophomore in college. She is pretty, as are her charming clothes; she looks one straight in the eyes when she talks, — hers are clear gray and have as much expression as those of a robin; and though it is plain to be seen that none of the things which make a

woman of one have touched her, she
has a calm assurance of bearing that
comes from perfect health. Health, indeed, shines out of her; her vitality
seems a force, and an almost overpow-
ering one. In her presence I feel myself small and shrunken of body. She
is the kind of capable modern girl who
knows how to make a parent mind, and
so compelling a quality is the serene
assurance of youth that I felt, as I sat
there beside Eliza Storrs, that, had
Gertrude been my daughter, I would
never have dared to face her with that
last year's plumage on my hat.

My own children and I have grown
up — I had almost said grown old —
together, and Margaret, while she may
scold me about my hat, will understand; but to Gertrude it will seem

mere wanton dowdiness, a sign of age
something akin to the losing of one's
faculties. This is because we have no
means of communication, as I found
out, to my surprise, when Gertrude
first arrived.

"How is your dear mother?" I
asked.

Gertrude told me, and then said that
they were all so glad at home that my
health was so much better than it had
been the winter before. I asked her
next how she liked college, and she replied she found it "broadening," and
then I asked her what her studies were.
I saw a little shadow of amusement
cross her face; and though she answered me with polite exactness, I
realized with chagrin that I had made
a mistake. I felt intellectually all el-

bows and feet, — they do not call them "studies" any more; young women of Gertrude's age speak about their "work" instead.

I find, as we grow old, we often repeat the experiences of our youth. As the world runs from me and I become less sure of my ground, I now and then have moments of extreme embarrassment in the presence of younger people — when my memory slips a cog, for instance, or when I find I have repeated the same thing twice — that is like nothing I have felt since when, as a little girl, I did things that made me long for the kindly earth to open and swallow me. The only difference is that now I can laugh off my mortification, and then I used to wash it away with tears.

After I had asked Gertrude about

her studies and she had answered, we seemed to have finished definitely and for all time everything we had to say to each other. We looked at each other kindly, even with a certain affection, but, nevertheless, conversation languished and died.

"Gertrude is a lovely girl, is n't she?" Margaret said to me later. "And so responsive!"—I had heard the two chattering away like a couple of magpies.

"Gertrude and I don't speak the same language," I answered, "though we're both tolerably proficient in the English tongue when we're not together."

"Not many young girls come to the house; perhaps that 's the reason," suggested Margaret.

"I'm sure," I replied, "I see a great deal of young people." For, you see, I thought it was all Gertrude's fault.

"A great deal of young people about thirty," said Margaret.

As I thought of my young friends, I found that Margaret was right; that while I had been asleep one night all my little girls that I was so proud of keeping in touch with had grown to be women "about thirty."

Since Gertrude came there have been plenty of real young people around the house. Margaret made a tea for her right away, and I had a chance to see the young people of my town, many of whom I am ready to take my oath were babies no later than day before yesterday, and I confess I still thought of them as babies. It is a long time

183

since I have recognized all the girls who bow to me on the street, for I am absent-minded, anyway. Now I am beginning to place a few of them. The pretty girl with curls is Laura Dickinson. I remember her at ten as an active pair of dividers careering over the earth's surface; I never saw a child with such thin, lively legs. The young man who pays Gertrude especial court is John Baker. I remember very well going to see him four days after he was born. He was Sarah Baker's first grandchild, and she was inordinately proud of him. After that, the last definite recollection I have of him is the time, when, at the age of five, he broke my china jar and yelled loudly with despair over what he had done. As they were named to me there was not one I

184

did not recall as a baby, and very few that I had n't taken for their older brothers and sisters.

How had they accomplished the process of growing up so fast, and where had they been when they were about it? That was the first thing that struck me. The next was how venerable I seemed to them. I am, as I have had occasion to mention before, what the people around here term a "mighty spry old lady," and noways infirm; but these children cannot remember a day when I was not old; they do not go back to the time when my hair was not already gray, and they give me the respect due to age. No one need tell me that among well-born young people the respect for the old is dead. These dear children fairly bristle with respect for me. If I come into the room where they are, they are full of charming little attentions in the way of easy-chairs, cushions, and footstools. Personally, I dislike soft-padded chairs. I was taught to sit upright as a girl, and I still sit so, my backbone being as strong as ever. I am never more uncomfortable than when I have several cushions tucked about me, but often of late years I have had to sit arranged in this modern way or seem ungracious. If women of Margaret's age frequently force sofa pillows on me, those of Gertrude's can hardly wait to say "good-afternoon" before they pop one behind me; old ladies and sofa cushions are in their minds inseparable.

The other day my old friend Eliza Storrs and I were coming home to-

gether in the electrics from Standish.
We had been on quite a jaunt together;
in fact, we had been to help each other
buy our new bonnets. We had had a
good time doing it, and came home
with that feeling of guilty triumph that
sweetened the disapproval which we
knew was before us.

"I suppose," Eliza admitted to me,
"that I shall never hear the last of it.
But," she added, with brisk decision
that was a sort of dress rehearsal of
the tone in which she would later say
the same thing to her daughter,—"*but*
there's no use talking about it *now*.
I've been to Standish and seen about
my hat, and I'm going again!"

Her tone had a triumphant trumpet-
ing quality to it. The truth of the matter was, Eliza had merely had three

187

new flowers and some foliage put in
her last year's bonnet; it had, further-
more, passed through the ambiguous
process known as "freshening up." For
my part, while I had indeed bought a
new hat, the trimming on my old one
being as good as new, I had used it
over again. It had been more expen-
sive in the beginning than I had intended to get; my daughter Margaret
was with me when I got it, and over-
persuaded me. So I, by using the last
year's trimming and Eliza Storrs her
last year's hat, had the feeling deep
down in our hearts that we had out-
witted our wise children, who are always trying to make us put more ex-
pensive things on our backs and heads
than there is any need for. I think that
older women often have the same guilty

joy, in spending less on themselves than they should, that young women do in being extravagant.

So, borne up by the feeling that is as exhilarating for a woman of seventy as for one of twenty-seven, — that of having done something she should not, — Eliza and I climbed into the electric car as light of foot as our years permitted. The car was full; we had barely entered it when two young girls, after giving each other a brief glance, sprang to their feet and hustled us into their seats. This kind act was accomplished promptly and thoroughly, and I would not for one moment be so ungracious as to give the impression that I was not grateful, nor would I for a moment undervalue the small kindnesses that the young so often shower on the old.

189

It was not their fault that the laughter died out of our eyes, and that our spirits flagged, and that even the triumph of having achieved a last year's hat seemed less amusing than it had a moment ago, while our young friends chattered as blithely, swaying to and fro as they held on to the straps, as they had before they gave us our seats.

You see, Eliza and I had taken a little vacation away from the Land of Old Age, — for there is nothing so rejuvenating as playing truant, and our day's excursion had been that, — and these young girls who had risen so promptly to give us their seats had led us back to our place in the world. We had forgotten for a moment that we belonged to the white-haired company who have won their right to a perpetual seat in the cars, and however welcome a seat may be, it is not so pleasant always to remember why it is our right.

I sat there watching them, and at last I asked Eliza: —

"What do you suppose they are talking about?"

"Something foolish," Eliza replied, without hesitation. "The way girls go on nowadays! When I was young, children and young people were supposed to let their elders do the talking, and now it's the young folks who do *all* the talking. I declare I sometimes feel as if I never had a chance to speak."

"Oh, come now, Eliza," said I. "You can't tell *me* that you've passed your life in a state of dumbness."

For Eliza has done her share of talking in this life.

I have known Eliza since we were schoolgirls together, and I tried to remember any concrete conversation that we had, as girls, in our endless gossiping together, and I found I could n't.

Throughout the ride the young girls did n't stop their talk for one moment, and went down the street still chatting, while I tried to piece out from the shreds my memory gave me the fabric of their conversation.

"Eliza," I said, "does it ever make you feel old when girls hop out of their seats in cars the minute they clap eyes on you?"

"Sometimes," Eliza admitted. "But," she added with decision, "it would make me feel a great deal older if I had had

192

to stand on my two feet all the way home from Standish!"

But while I might not wish to stand so long, I would gladly do without some of the small attentions by which I am fairly snowed under the moment I come among them. And this is not the only thing that happens when I appear. Conversation stops. They go on talking, to be sure, but I know they are talking with me for an audience, and that they expurgate their talk as they go along, just as older people's talk insensibly changes when a child of twelve joins them; just as I have weeded my talk a hundred times out of respect to the young, these dear children weed their talk from respect to the old. I am aware that they have a very vivid idea of what I think the conduct and con-

193

versation of young people ought to be, and as far as they can they instinctively conform to it — when I am around. It is taken for granted not only by these very young people, but by my older young friends my daughter's age, that by virtue of my years I am a conservative, and that I am deeply pained by certain phases of modern life. It is true that I should not like to see a woman smoke, and I wish that young girls were less slangy and noisy on the street; but I realize that each generation will have phases which seem unlovely to the older generation. So, while I may have opinions of my own at variance with those of the present day, I am not as hopelessly conservative as I seem in the presence of Gertrude and her friends. I would be glad for the courage to tell

194

them that I would rather be shocked than have this well-meant little farce played for me, but this I shall never dare, for I shall never know them well enough.

Perhaps it is the fault of us older women that the young people are so careful of our feelings. It must be that we have ourselves put so much distance between us and them. There are some of us who are too eager to tell how well-behaved we were when we were young; who have too much to say about the slovenly ways young people have of standing and sitting, and of their slangy ways of speaking, for us to meet them often on a comfortable footing. We older women have less criticism for the younger ones than older women had formerly, I think. I fancy that to-day our attitude is one easier to get on with. I don't believe I hear so much about girls being "giddy" as I used to when I was a young girl. So perhaps by the time Gertrude is an old woman the young people of her day won't be as afraid of saying something she will disapprove of as she is. Still, if she is one of those of us who don't take everything for granted, she will find the way back to her girlhood a long one.

One does n't need to reach the Land of Old Age to smile over the things that caused one's despair when one was Gertrude's age; so it is n't to be wondered at that the dust of years obliterates all trace of the things we laughed over and cried over so long ago. And yet, while I know that the things that

seem important to Gertrude seem un-
important to me, and will be unimpor-
tant to her five years from now, by
virtue of her youth and health she can
make me feel my years. She can set
me wondering about the girl I once
was, and I sometimes have a vague
shame that I remember so little.

When I look at the young girls chattering in the street, I can only wonder
about what they are talking; I knew
once, now I have forgotten, and there
is nothing that can make me remember.
If Gertrude lived here, we should get
to be very good friends, and in spite
of the mutual embarrassment we now
cause each other, we should find a va-
riety of things to say to each other,
plenty of common ground on which to
meet. Then, too, every day Gertrude

would be growing older, she would be coming nearer to my point of view, and very soon we should come to understand each other, — and I should wake up to find that Gertrude was thirty and married, with a couple of babies.

CHAPTER X

UNSPOKEN WORDS

As soon as a young girl marries and turns into a mother, then there is that in the hearts of all of us older women which speaks to her, for among the most poignant things in our memories is the love that we bore our little children and the mistakes we made in the rearing of them.

There is a great pathos to me in the young mothers who try so earnestly to do what is best ; for, however we bring up our children, we are sure to make irreparable mistakes, and as we old people look back over the long road we have traveled, we see that it has been watered by the needless tears we have shed, and worse still, those we have made our children shed because of our needless severities. Whether we were firm or whether we were lenient, we are sure to regret the course we took ; for there is no mother living who at the end of her life would bring up her children over again in the same way, nor one who does not believe in her heart that she could do better a second time.

We have realized how futile our own theories of " governing children " are, and that there is very little mothers can do for their children besides trying humbly to understand them and to avoid injustices. I don't think it is possible for any mother to do more, but it is possible to do a great deal less. So those of us who have gotten to a place where certain parental firmnesses seem tyranny, and certain sorts of discipline cruelty, would be glad to have their daughters learn this before it is too late.

᾽ I remember so vividly a recent struggle Margaret had with Betty that was so like one of those I had with her. Betty and I were sitting together on the piazza. We were singing. I take solid comfort singing with Betty, for as I grow older I find it very pleasant to have some one in the world who does n't notice how thin and wavering my notes are, and who likes to listen to my voice, worn as it is. Presently Margaret joined us.

"Mother," Betty asked, "may I go down to Annie's house — "

"No; I can't let you go to-day,"

interrupted Margaret ; and though she spoke gently, her answer came with such promptness I knew Betty's question was a cue she had been waiting for.

"Why not ?" came Betty's little whine—that sad little "Why not ?" that every mother of us knows so well.

"Because you didn't come home when I told you to yesterday."

"But I *told* Annie I'd come—"

"Well, I tell you you can't," replied my daughter cheerfully.

You know what happened then, don't you ? There were tears and teasing. Margaret was firm. Betty was persistent. Margaret told Betty to stop crying and Betty cried the harder. I gathered through her sobs that there was to have been lemonade. As Margaret still refused, Betty grew defiant. I opened my mouth to say something, and then decided not to. If all the words, for only one day, which a mother of my generation *does n't* say to her middle-aged children, were gathered together, they would make instructive reading.

At last Margaret led Betty away, saying gently, " Dear, I only keep you in because I must"; and then she ended with a reproachful, " Oh, why do you make me punish you ?" Which was her way of saying the old " It hurts me more than it does you."

Soon Margaret came back and sat down by me. We could hear Betty sobbing upstairs.

" The worst of it is," said Margaret, " she thinks I'm unjust."

We rocked back and forth, and for

203

a while neither of us spoke. Little wandering airs blew the long trailing vine of the creeper to and fro. We presented to the passers-by the same spectacle of peace that Betty and I had a few moments before. But we two knew how changed things were, for the only sound in the world that we heard was that persistent, angry sobbing upstairs. I knew that Margaret's heart was wrung with it, and I suffered with her, for Margaret is my baby, and very mercifully we cannot suffer for our grandchildren's tears, or any other tears, for that matter, as we do for those of our own children.

Besides, while I was sorry for Betty, —and I will tell you privately that my sympathies were with her, though I wouldn't have confessed it to Margaret, — I was glad to see the little thing show so much spirit. She was protesting with all her strength against what seemed to her injustice and the abuse of power; — and you can feel these things with as great indignation as any one, even though you are not old enough to call them by their names. And so, though I hate to hear a child cry, if it had n't been for Margaret's distressed face, I should have had a certain satisfaction in hearing Betty's indignant roars.

As a baby Betty was *too* good. Margaret brought her up in the modern, cast-iron, systematic way, and her subdued whimpers of useless protest went to my heart; I used to find myself wishing she would have a good old-fashioned fit of crying, with yells that one could hear across the street. So it was a relief, as Betty grew older, to have her show a normal amount of strong will, although Margaret has been as perplexed as if the nursery clock had up and defied her. I have never dared tell Margaret how I felt about this, for there is nothing that irritates a mother of the present generation more than to have her own mother give her advice concerning the rearing of children, however much experience she may have had. Like most grandmothers of to-day, I have wisely held my tongue, though sometimes it has been hard work not to speak.

Margaret was learning that while you may make rules for a baby, there is no set of rules made by man that will apply to a child of six, for Betty

continued to sob defiantly. At last
Margaret said: —

"I have to make her mind, you
know."

I nodded.

"She must learn to keep her prom-
ises."

"Of course," I assented. Poor girl,
I knew she was making apologies to
herself for causing Betty unhappiness.

"If I had known she cared so
much — "

I nodded again. I knew so well what
she felt. I also knew what I would do
if I were in her place; because one is a
mother is no reason why one shouldn't
retire gracefully from a false position.

"But now I can't, of course — " she
concluded firmly.

Again I outwardly agreed, — this

is one of the arts one acquires with years, — but what I wanted to say was: —

"Why not? Why can't you give in?"

One of the tenets of the governing of children is that when you have made a mistake, have given a too heavy punishment or imposed a command that is more distasteful than you dreamed it would be, you must persist in the matter to the end. We deal this way with our children, little and big, and unreasonable obstinacy is called "being firm." Why we feel we must act this way, I don't know. I have never known, even when I was most "firm" myself, and I don't believe any one else does. I'm sure Margaret did n't. We were silent again.

"If one could only know what one ought to do. Oh, it's so hard to know what's right!" sighed my poor daughter at last.

In the past half-hour she had gone over the weary path every mother must travel so often. We mete out to our children what seems like justice, but justice turns its back on us and leaves us stranded with a child who is crying its eyes out because it is unjustly treated. As Margaret said, — "It is so hard to know what is right."

So old women who see their little grandchildren playing about them cannot help but think of their own lost babies. Out of the past our little children look at us, and as our eyes meet theirs we falter: —

"My child, I did the best I knew."

"Yes, mother." — Then, "Mother, do you remember the time you laughed at me, and because I got angry you punished me?"

You say meekly: —

"I was rude that time, and then unjust, dear."

"Mother, do you remember —"

But you can't bear to listen. You know how many times you didn't do your best; the times you were gentle because you were too cowardly to fight; the times when you punished without understanding; the times when you imposed too heavy penalties for childish faults — for, after all, you were no better mother than you were woman; and so you change your boast of having done your best to: —

"My child, I loved you dearly always — through your mistakes and through mine."

That is the most that any mother of us can say. As we grow old, we are very apt to return in spirit to the days when our children were our very own, and wonder we did n't treasure them more. We find out, as we get along in years, that we could have been just as good mothers with fewer tears shed.

I cannot bear to think how I made Margaret and Helen sleep on little hard nubbins of curl-papers so they might have fluffy curls the next day,— curls were the fashion then, and my children had hair as straight as a string. I hate to remember how I forced them to eat the things they did n't want to. I had a long battle with Helen over soft-boiled eggs; she would not eat

211

them. No one was benefited by my persistence, nor could possibly have been, whichever way the battle came out; it was of no importance either way; but I made the whole household uncomfortable with the conflict. I didn't believe, in those days, in "humoring children about their food." Dear me! How many needless tears I made that child shed, and how unhappy I was over it! I thought eggs were for Helen's good, and I was bound she should eat them. I am glad to remember that in the end she won, and I can only look back and wonder at myself for my foolish persistence.

I sometimes wake up in the night and think over some of the little unkindnesses I did Margaret, or some coveted pleasure I denied my children because it was too much trouble to let them do as they wanted, and I have the same bitter regret over these things, small though they seemed at the time, that I might have had if I had lost my babies through death instead of losing them only by having them grow up into men and women. Every older woman has a sad little collection of such memories. They are among the few sad things one carries with one to the end of life, for age does not make us forget our injustices towards our little children. We remember them always, and time, instead of softening them, makes them grow worse. Incidents that in youth seemed of little importance look very much like cruelties when we look at them from the Land of Old Age.

So I was glad when Margaret could stand it no longer and went upstairs to Betty. As she went into the room, the child burst into a fresh storm of tears. Margaret tried tenderly to calm her ; but it was freedom or nothing for Betty.

So Margaret said things like : "You know you never get things by crying for them. — Betty ! If you speak so to me I shall have to punish you severely ! "

She came downstairs again with a firm line around her mouth. I knew just how she felt. She had gone into battle, and she intended to fight it out to the end, — whether it was good for Betty or not. I looked at Margaret and I felt that time had gone backward, and that Margaret was myself and Betty one of my own children, while I myself was some invisible outsider watching

214

the same old conflict repeat itself.
Most older women, as they watch their
grown-up children, have this almost
uncanny feeling of living over again
their own mistakes and blunders. At
such times one cannot help an obscure
feeling of responsibility, as if somehow
it were one's own fault, so much are
your daughter's mistakes your very
own ; at such times I cannot keep from
trying to help, even though I know it
is unwise, so I had to say at last : —

"Don't you think you are making a
great deal out of a small matter?"

It was such a miserable way of wast-
ing a bit of one's childhood and youth.

"Disobedience is n't a small matter,"
replied Margaret shortly.

"Carelessness is," I suggested.

"She's a very obstinate child!"

Margaret asserted. By this time she had lost sight of the fact that it was the sense of injustice that made Betty obstinate.

Then, as I started to say something more : —

" Darling," Margaret interrupted with awful patience, " I 've got to fight this out myself. You 're only making it harder for me."

I had it on my lips to say : " It would be better for you if you allowed your mother to make a suggestion now and then ! " For no one likes to be asked to hold one's tongue, however politely, and above all by one's own child. But as I looked at Margaret's careworn young face, and saw her plodding along the iron path she called duty, — in this case, as in so many

216

others, a path which led nowhere, —
my little flash of impatience died.

But my spirit cried out to her though
my lips did n't speak: —

"Oh, my dear, it's no matter at all!
Don't, don't feel so about it!"

Then I went away, leaving Margaret
making her tragic mountain out of
Betty's little molehill of carelessness ;
remembering in my young days how
warmly I sympathized with a friend
of mine whose mother always interfered
in the discipline of her little grandson.
Whatever he had done, "How happy
he was before you disturbed him!" she
would say, reproachfully.

Now I understand. There are so
many sorrows and cares which we
must inevitably meet as we journey
toward age, and so many perplexing

217

moments in life which we cannot avoid, that we want, oh, so much, that our children might at least be spared and spare themselves the unnecessary worries. It is the useless mistakes and needless suffering each generation undergoes that we of the older protest against, and for which we now and then break silence, only to learn again the bitter lesson of our uselessness.

CHAPTER XI

I COULD N'T help Margaret that day in that one little thing any more than I have been able to help my children in the greater crises of life. I could n't even imagine I was helping her; and this is one of the bitterest things we mothers have to bear when we get old. We have learned then that we can't help our children to lead their lives one bit better. There is not one single little stone we can clear from before their feet, be our old fingers ever so willing. With yearning hearts we see them making the mistakes we could teach them to avoid if only they would listen. We see them going through one

experience after another, — stumbling
here; again hurting themselves against
the same corner you hurt yourself
against so long ago; repeating all the
world-worn mistakes, while we elders
watch anxiously and may not even cry
out, — "Take care!" Our sons repeat
the follies of their fathers; our daughters make over again all the mistakes
of their mothers. It is very hard to sit
in silence when you see them doing all
the things that you did and then so
painfully learned better. We feel that
we could so easily point to the fair
open road if our children would let us,
but we are as useless to them as guide-
posts to the blind. We must watch our
children lose themselves in the tangle
whose miseries we know so well, and
see them at last, after long years of

wandering, find their way back home,
heart-sore and worn; — and all the time
we can't help thinking it all need n't
have been. That, to us older mothers,
is the heart-rending part of it. Instead
of helping, you must sit quiet and fold
your hands, knowing that if you did
speak they would n't hear you. Your
children, however dearly they love you,
will think you say what you do only
because you are old and have forgotten, and therefore you cannot possibly
understand life as they see and live it.
If you run after your children crying,
"Oh, my child, don't do this," they
won't listen to you, or if they do they
smile at you as if you were a child.
They are so sure, these young people,
they know more about life than you
do! Or it may very well be that in-

stead of smiling, they have hard work not to show you how impatient they are that you have interfered in something you can't know about.

The right of free speech with our children is one of the pleasures of life which age often takes from us. When they are young they listen, — they have to then, even if they go away and forget; but as they get older, they don't often let us have the illusion that we are listened to. I have even known some mothers who were not allowed to talk at all about their children's interests.

I have never understood the watchful irritation with which our grown children meet our suggestions concerning their affairs, for these are the things that lie nearest our hearts. Are

222

they afraid, I wonder, that we will forget they are grown up? I grant it sometimes is hard to act as if one realized it.

However this may be, there are very few grown people who can bear advice from their own mothers, even though they listen patiently to all the rest of the world. I remember I had the same curious intolerance for my mother's advice, and now I am at a loss to account for my impatience. Did I fancy, I wonder, that my problems were so different from those she had solved during her long life?

There are, after all, few mothers who have grown old in the service of their children who have not some little wisdom ready to give. Some of us have learned a short road to peace; all of

223

us have learned something that would make life easier for the children we love, but out of the fullness of our knowledge and experience we can give away not so much as a crumb. That evening I almost envied Margaret her trying afternoon; she believed, for the moment anyway, that she was doing her Betty good.

There is something very touching in the unreasonable expectation each generation has for its children. Obedience, cheerfulness, self-control, punctuality, are only a few of the virtues every young mother starts out by expecting of her babies. It only shows the serene self-confidence the young have in making the next generation better than the last. For, mind you, every mother expects to do this herself, and it's a happy

time when you still have the illusion of
power and still believe you can play
Providence for your children, that you
can bring them up very much as you
choose ; when you still feel that everything depends on you, and that with
your love for them you will be able to
defend them, not only from the world
but from themselves. And so for a very
little while you can. Young mothers in
their tender ignorance imagine that
this will always be so.

But very soon your children slip from
between your fingers. They develop
new traits that you don't understand and
others you understand only too well,
for like weeds your own faults come up
and refuse to be rooted out, and you lie
awake nights trying "to know what is
right," still thinking that your child's

225

welfare is in your own hand, trying with your own little strength to combat faults that are as old as your race, that are part of you and your mother and her mother before you, and will be part of your children's children. I see my daughters going valiantly to work at this hopeless task, high in courage, full of confidence that *their* children shall be saved anyway. As they bring their children up, they often talk to me about their own childhood, — and very tenderly point out the mistakes I made with them. I smile one of those inward smiles age knows so well, as I gather from their accent, more than from anything they say, that they hope to avoid all my errors ; and indeed that they think they have avoided a good many already.

I let them talk. The last time Henry was on a visit we talked of old times and old methods, and especially of the desultory education I gave Margaret. Henry is doing better in this respect, and my older granddaughters are on the road to becoming very learned young ladies. I only hope Henry is taking as much pains to make his girls stand up straight as I did with her. While we compared new educational methods with the faulty old ones, I could n't help saying to my daughter : " All I hope, dear, is that when you 're my age you will have as devoted a set of children."

For when your children have disproved all your theories ; when none of your sons have taken up the professions you tried so hard to have them ; when

227

they have consulted their own wills in everything in life, their affection is the great recompense. If our children really love us and show us that they do, I think we may count that we have won in the game of life, and I would be glad to have my children realize this, and have it help them over the discouragement of those years after their children have apparently slipped from them altogether.

When I was a young mother I believed, too, that I could be a Providence for my children. I believed they had been given me to mould as I would, and the only limit of the influence I would have was the limit of my own strength and love. Then there came a time when I realized that every child on the street my child stopped to talk with had its share in bringing up my sons and daughters. One week in school was enough to upset all the training of years. They learned faster from their friends, and more willingly, than ever they did from me, and it seemed to me then that they learned the things they ought n't to quickest of all. My well-brought-up little boys came from play talking loudly, making faces, playing the fool. Margaret would come home from a visit with a trunkful of affectations and an assortment of silly ideas, — how silly I knew very well, for I had had those same ideas and thrown them aside myself; why I did n't get comfort out of the fact that I had outgrown these very things, and that they, too, would in time inevitably outgrow them, I don't know. It's a bad moment when one realizes that the most shallow boy and girl can have an influence over your children greater than your own, and that some thoughtless ridicule from any one your sons admire is able to undo all your patient work. It was when I saw these things that I began to see that my place in my children's lives must be very much less than I had first supposed, but I only redoubled my efforts. By that time I was past the place when commands and punishments were very much used. I used all my tact and affection and diplomacy to make my children what I wanted them.

As they grew older still, I found my ideals of what I wanted them modified and changed by what they were. How much I am responsible for what they are to-day I am at a loss to decide, but

I do know that the boy next door has always had a more direct and apparently a stronger influence than I ever had.

However philosophical I might be, however glibly I talked to myself about "heredity and environment," I felt deep down in my heart that I was responsible, and I alone, for what my children were. How many hours I have spent — yes, and days and months — in wondering just how I had failed. I felt that I was responsible for every one of their faults, that with more wisdom and more courage and more patience everything might have been different.

I have always envied those women who can say, " Anna gets her obstinacy from her father's family," or, " George

231

has the Crawford temper"; but perhaps they too feel, down deep in their hearts, that they are somehow to blame for whatever is wrong. I was already an old woman before I was able to free myself of my part of the burden of responsibility, for in the end I realized that, after all, I could n't hold myself accountable for the things that happened when they were away from me altogether. But always the torturing question remains with us mothers, "If I had done differently, could I have saved my daughter this unhappiness? If I had been firmer, could n't I have helped my son more?"

It makes no difference what good children you have or how well they have "turned out"; mothers still ask themselves these questions, so heavily do the sins of their children weigh on them, even when they are not sins at all. I have always wondered why nothing has ever been said about the sins of the children being visited on the parents, for if our sins are visited on our children theirs are doubly hard for us to bear. After they have forgotten them we still remember, for we wonder always if we might not have prevented them by greater wisdom.

As one advances farther into the Land of Old Age, one sees more and more how isolated each generation is from the other. We begin, like Margaret, playing Providence to our children. We end, like myself, a spectator at the drama of our children's lives. You will not be able to turn the tragedy into a comedy. You can only watch it, breathless, no more able to stop the march of events than the little boy in the gallery who hisses the villain. If we mothers have helped at all, it is what we are, and not what we have taught, that has counted. Yet, though we older people know there is a gulf of time between our children and us that may not be bridged, we can't help trying to bridge it.

If you are in the thick of the play of life, look around you and you will see the gray-headed spectators who have themselves stepped off the stage. They are the mothers and fathers of the players, and each one of them is murmuring advice or encouragement to some dear child who never stops to listen. Some cry as they look on, and some laugh, and some sit proud and complacent, and in her heart each one of them knows that the words she repeats so often are not heard. But they keep on, for deeper than the knowledge of their own uselessness is the feeling of responsibility. You must bear the sins of your children until you die, just as you have your silent part in their successes. You put them in the world and you feel that you must answer to yourself for what they are.

Though each generation must work out its own salvation, we mothers can't reconcile ourselves to this knowledge. To our last days many of us go on persisting in the belief that we could help our grown-up children if they would only stop long enough to listen.

In spite of myself, I believe this. I can't help it, and I like to think that they listen more than either of us knows, and that because they love me so dearly, they hear, after all, the things I don't speak out loud. So at the end of life I can only say to myself what I wanted to say to Margaret: Each one of us can help her children, she her small ones and I my big ones, only by loving them dearly and trying humbly to understand; for I believe that only in this way can one generation come near to the other.

CHAPTER XII

I HAVE spoken of us older people
as spectators at the play of life, speaking words of encouragement which
were not heard; and if we speak words
that are not heard, so are our ears almost always on the alert to catch the
inner meaning of our children's lives,
to enter in and understand all the details that are kept from us.

I have a son whom I have seen but
few times in many years; he lives in a
distant country and can seldom come
home. I have pictures of the house in
which he lives. Often his face shines
out to me familiarly from a strange
group of people, none of whose faces I

237

know. Often it will be a little snap-
shot, and from the looks and gestures
arrested in the photograph, I will see
that they are friends of his. Once in a
while word comes that "this is So-and-
So, you know," or that "the lady beside me is Miss This or Miss That,"
— nothing more. I am familiar with all
the outer surfaces of his life, as though
I had lived out there with him. Every
morning and evening when I pray for
my children I go, it seems to me, almost bodily out toward him in that
inner communion that we must feel
when we pray intensely for those whom
we love. In all the years of our sepa-
ration no woman has had a more faithful child. Week after week his letters
come — full letters, too; I follow him in
his small journeys, in his comings and

goings. I hear the old man and wife talk, that have done for him for so long, and to whose quaint picturesqueness he never becomes accustomed beyond the point of appreciation. I know his tastes and his pleasures and his recreations. I know that materially he is doing well, but of his inner life, of his defeats, of his triumphs, of his travail in the stuff of his own character, I know nothing except what any one might know, — that he is a good fellow, sweet-tempered, as he always was, and that he has a certain touch of arrogance, of kind-hearted authority in his air that is not unlike Dudley's. Any one might know this who saw his picture or who heard him spoken of. But he might be going through the crisis of his life even, with his spirit in deep distress, and I am sure he would sit down, from force of habit, and write me one of his chatty and entertaining letters that make up a part of my life. If he is ill, you may be sure I hear nothing of it until he is better.

Since he cannot be with me in body it should be enough for me, I suppose, that he is in spirit with me enough so that he turns to me and gives me so much of his time. Yet it is not enough; it leaves me hungry. I never read one of his kind and charming letters without wondering: "Is all well with you, my son? Is life kind to you? Are your days lonely? Does the lack of wife and children press heavily upon you, or is the crust of selfishness settling over you so that you would not sell your small freedom of personal habits for the great gift of love which wife and children would give you? Is the blight of middle age creeping upon you, swallowing up the generosities of your youth that I knew so well? Or is your heart hungry for those children that you have never had, and is there some face dear to you beyond all others, so for want of it you must lead your life lonely as you do now?" These questions have never been answered for me, nor will they be ever. Yet sometimes it seems to me that I know as much of him as I do about those two children who have strayed familiarly through these desultory pages. They, too, are as careful to turn to me the smiling side of their lives as my son so far away from me.

It is perhaps for this that I feel nearer to my son Henry than to any of my

children. He writes me seldom and then
only brief communications. My knowledge of his life and comings and goings
is through my daughter-in-law, but in
the nature of his business he makes me
brief and flying visits; he descends upon
us at odd moments, which disturbs Margaret and Dudley. They try and try to
make him telegraph me or write when
he is coming. They think his unexpected
visits disturb me; I suppose they get
this from my trembling eagerness at the
times when I am surprised into saying: "I think Henry is coming to-
night."

And very often he comes when I think
he is, and then again I am wrong, though
I am superstitious enough to believe
that he has thought of coming and then
changed his mind when this strong feel-

242

ing of his nearness sweeps over me. And when he comes I see him as he is. If he has made a good business deal or if business worries him, he says so, while Dudley and Margaret hover around like two anxious parents, trying to play Providence. If they know he is coming, they meet him first with warnings and head-shakings, coaching him what to tell me and what not to tell me; and for a time he tries to be good, but before he goes, he flings out to me what is worrying or troubling him. To him I speak my mind more than to any one, and preach to him the self-control that he needs. He comes to me as he has always come, for a certain sort of strength. I give him balance and smooth him out. I am to him what I am not to any of my other children,— the mother of younger years; the mother

243

to whom to turn for advice and strength,
and I leap out to meet it.

My other children — those who see
me from day to day — tell me that his
visits upset me, and so they do. I have
been ill and depressed sometimes for
two or three days when I have not been
able to get him, or when his worry has
been a difficult one, as I always was ;
as I was when they were ill ; as I was
through the difficult phases in the boys'
developments.

Tranquillity and peace perhaps pro-
long life, and yet — who knows ?
There seems to be before us the question as to whether we shall wear out
or rust out, and most of us are praying
to fate that we may be allowed to wear
out. Yet who can judge ? I know that
my children's silence, at which I often

chafe, is not best for me, but perhaps it is best for them, since I cannot help them, since my anxiety only heightens theirs. When I see them cloaking their troubles with smiles ; when I feel the atmosphere surcharged with anxiety, and see the cloud lift again, I often think it is perhaps self - preservation that makes them do what they call " spare me " ; that to watch me troubled and broken with anxiety about their worries would be for them a double strain.

I know when Betty was ill that my trouble — though I was tranquil and though I spoke heartening words — was an added burden to Margaret. I know that for her there were two sick people in the house ; that I was one, ill and suffering spirit for the sick body

245

of her child. And while it seems to me that silence is perhaps the hardest of all to bear, the peace it brings is good for all of us.

I have said that we should decide whether we should rust out or wear out, but perhaps that was decided for us in our youth and in our middle age, for we are continually deciding all our life long what kind of old people we are to be. Every moment of our lives we are preparing for age ; carving out the faces that we are to wear ; moulding and modeling and casting our characters for good or for bad ; deciding if those last years — those dependent years, so full of heartbreak, so full of the giving-up of those things which make life life— shall be bearable to those closest to us.

Some years ago I began observing

the various types of age about me, and it appeared to me in many unlovely guises. Often the women whom life had treated the most gently turned toward life unlovely faces, — masks of discontent. I ask myself, Is life so sad that on the faces of age one should so often see such deep prints of ineradicable grief, or is it the habit of discontent, year by year, planting a wrinkle here and drawing down the mouth there ?

I, who am as yet only what people call elderly, look sometimes with a certain fright at the faces which I see that are old. I see upon the street old men whose faces are carven as though in granite ; the hardness of their own hard hearts is there in every line. Others I see yet more terrible, — loose-mouthed and vacant-eyed, speaking of

a life of indulgence of the body. They
have no thoughts to carry with them to
the grave ; no light from the hills makes
them lift up their eyes ; they have forgotten the hills if ever they knew them.
And the faces of the old women, — how
vacant are so many of them ; how dis-
contented! What furrowed brows,
penned with sorrow as though their
thoughts had become steeped with sadness until it had become moulded on
every line of the face without. What
bitterness again! And all these things
bespeak a feebleness of the spirit.
Day by day, as they walk on the road
that leads to age, they forge out of
life their own masters and the doom of
those about them as well. There is
something in character that seems to
survive even the mind. I often call to

mind the story of Emerson, who, when his mind failed and he could n't think of words and what he wanted to say, waited with a sublime patience, —sometimes waited for the word that would n't come. His own serenity outlived the worn-out tool that had used it for such high purposes.

I remember from the days of my early middle life an old woman who had become completely childish and rambled around the town in which she lived, a harmless and fantastic figure. Deafness was added to her other infirmities. And yet, as she went along the streets talking to herself, one caught snatches of a mind imperishably enwrapped in the kind things of life.

"What a beautiful child!" one would

hear her remark. "Oh, the lovely child! . . . What a lovely day!"

This poor distraught and maimed spirit saw beauty everywhere. She would stop a stranger on the street to know if she knew the Mrs. Grant with whom she lived. "Such a beautiful woman! So good, so good!"

Of all the lessons that come to me out of my past, the lesson of this creature, never a stalwart spirit, but, like her friend, "so good," returns to me the oftenest. She had had a heart that had been a fountain of love to all that came near her; though she had never been a woman of much brains or wisdom, yet her indestructible sweetness survived her, and this, it seems to me, is the lesson that age should bring to youth continually.

"Choose," says Age, "this face so beneficent, so sweet, so kind, or this other, written over and over with the small, mean vices of uncharitableness and littleness."

This much is to a certain degree in our hands, but what is not in our hands is the final end, the terrible and inevitable breaking-up of the powers of the body; the end that no one can tell if it shall come swiftly and mercifully or with torment for those one loves and for one's self. One can only hope here; one cannot know. And I suppose it is because of this menace that glides before us more and more closely, if we stop to think, that so many older men and women have such impatience at having clipped from them one or any of the little things that still make life the place it was. Every outer sign of age reminds us of this; every new feebleness of the body brings before us vividly the goal to which we are tending, — not the goal of death, but perhaps the goal of the last years of an enfeebled and broken and useless life. I think it is this shadow that chills the hearts of those of us who have brave spirits more than the thought of death.

CHAPTER XIII

GROWING OLD GRACEFULLY

I REMEMBER very well indeed when I began to hate to look at myself in the glass. That is the turning-point, — I hated to look at myself. The women who look in the glass oftenest are not the vainest ones. Where a woman looks in the glass out of vanity once, she looks in the glass twenty times as a matter of criticism, — looks to see if her hat is on straight, looks to see if her belt is doing its duty, looks to see if her skirt hangs well.

There came a time in my life when, while I was no longer young, I had a wholesome middle-aged look. I was no

better looking and no worse than my
neighbors, and my children encouraged
vanity in me, as one's dear children very
often will, by saying the sweet and familiar words : "How dear you look to-
day, mother ! I love to see mother in
that dress "; or, admonishing me ; "Mother, you really must have a new hat.
Look at mother's hat ! "

The moment comes to every woman
when, instead of flushing under the ap-
proval of some masculine creature, —
either sweetheart or husband, according
to her state of life, she sees herself mirrored in the eyes of her grown - up
children. You may be sure that these
little children of yours, that you see
now growing up around you, will in time
pay you more tribute and also give you
more frank criticism than any one you

have ever known, devoted husband or sweetheart as he may have been.

I wear certain laces and a certain brooch because my son Dudley cares for them, certain colors because of my daughter Margaret, and I am continually in a state of border warfare with them both for trying to make me buy new things which I do not need and that are clear beyond my pocketbook. And my case is the same as that of many an elderly woman of my acquaintance ; we have to fairly fight with our children not to put every penny we possess upon our backs. No young lady just coming out could hear the words from loving relatives that she needs a new dress so often as I do.

I will come back to what I was saying, — there was a time in my life when

because of the flattery of those I loved
— and there is no flattery more far-
reaching than that — I surveyed my
middle-aged reflection in the glass with
peace of heart. One of my daughters
would inform me that she thought I was
the prettiest mother in the world; the
blessed part of it is, I think they really
believed this was true. Then the day
came when I realized that my face was
old. I had been out of health, nothing
very serious or alarming, but I had lost
flesh and had n't been out of doors much,
and one day as I turned to meet my reflection it seemed to me that a thousand
wrinkles started out at me, that there
were lines about my eyes, that my whole
face was shrunken.

People speak of the terrible moment
it is in a woman's life when she finds

her first wrinkle. I don't believe most normal women find the first wrinkle at all. Very few of us are professional beauties ; the happiness of very few of us consists in our staying in our first flush of looks forever. The average, normal, comfortable woman is too busy looking after her babies and her home about the time the first wrinkle puts in an appearance to even notice it, and, even if she does, to be disturbed, because all her contemporaries are no better off than she. The discovery of age is a different thing. I don't know if all women realize from one day to another as I do this creeping on of the hands of Time, but I think there must come a day of definite awakening. I have seen women stricken down with some illness and go to bed plump and

257

middle-aged, and emerge, a few weeks afterwards, from the sick-room, frosted with age. I have seen sorrow rob women of the Indian summer of youth still more often. Generally it comes upon them stealthily like a thief in the night; you don't know how long it has been coming on, but little by little you find yourself " Old Mrs. So-and-So " instead of " Mrs. So-and-So."

The first wrinkle when one has children and a loving husband means nothing at all, but this look of age—it is the first cold warning of the Valley of the Shadow, it is a sign that one is actually on the road downhill, that the best days of life are over, that the activities that have made life worth living, from now on must slip more and more from one's fingers. My heart may feel as young as

ever, but what good is that if my knees
are rusty and going up and down stairs
begins to be a burden, and I find myself
tired after a little walk, and I know that
never again can I go back, that not one
of these wrinkles can vanish with returning health, that activities once given up
have gone from us then forever.

Small wonder then that I don't like
to look at my face, though it is still
sweet in the eyes of my children. I don't
like, I frankly confess, to be reminded
of all that the wrinkles and gray hair
imply. There is no vanity in this: I
never was enough of a beauty to be vain
about my looks, but was always glad
that I could be, as my unflattering aunts
used to say when I was a little girl,
" well enough," and that "I would pass
in a crowd." I think, indeed, I am better

looking as an older woman than as a
younger one. My features are of the
kind that endure, my hair has taken a
not unpleasing shade of gray, and yet
I turn from this reflection of a not ill-
looking elderly woman, not because I
mind being older, but because now and
then it comes quickly to me to what age
and to what goal I am so fast approaching. The spacious and sunny hours, occupations to my liking, and my dear
children at hand to smooth the road for
me, make life a pleasant place, — so I
turn my face away.

Not long ago there was visiting some
neighbors of ours an elderly relative.
Her hair had not turned gray, but had
kept a rather nondescript fluffy blond.
She had also retained what is called
" the figure of a girl." I expect that in

reality she was a fairly angular woman under her successful millinery; anyway she lacked the comfortable roundness that comes to most women who do not grow thin with advancing years, and for my part I had rather resemble a comfortable armchair than a little spidery bent-wood affair that looks as if it would blow away in a good strong wind. This woman, however, at a little distance, gave a sad little illusion of youth. As one saw her going down the street, for instance, one would have thought her quite a young person; across the room one would have given her forty-five, — forty-five dressed with a certain discreet youthfulness; and close at hand she looked very young for her age, very well preserved. This caused a good deal of comment.

"Well," said Margaret, "I'm glad you don't look like that, mother! I think it is absurd for a woman of her age with middle-aged daughters to dress the way she does."

"Yes," returned one of our neighbors, "and do you notice her complexion? It seems to me," went on this young mentor of the aged, "that women don't know how to grow old gracefully the way they used to."

I said nothing, but my heart went out to this poor lady who was struggling so valiantly to shove back the hands of the clock; and I would like to make here a little plea to you younger people. I know it is considered becoming to do what is called "grow old gracefully"; that is, to face the world with all your wrinkles, to have the courage of your

262

gray hairs, to lay aside your favorite
gay colors and put on the dark colors
in which people are supposed most
suitably to mourn their dead youth; I
know that younger people consider that
we should be willing and eager even to
betray every one of the years we have
lived by our actions, by our looks, by
our dress, and I do not pretend that
this is not the bravest part to take, but
here and there we find a coward in this
world, and let us not be untender. Who
knows what pressure has been brought
to bear? It is silly, if you like, it is lack-
ing in intelligence to try to hide one's
age, but what a tragedy it confesses,
what a futile and heart-rending struggle!
When I see women, as I have in the
past, with foolish false fronts which
did n't match their grizzling back hair,

when I see youthful garments on old shoulders, I am sometimes filled with impatience and think, "Oh, you silly woman!" But I am still more filled with pity and say, "Poor woman! Sad woman! Woman on whose shoulders so heavy a burden has been laid that you cannot face the inevitable!"

I remember there lived in our town a maiden lady who kept her pretty looks so that she was like a sort of thistle-down wraith of a girl. She lived alone and on so small a stipend that no one knew how she kept soul and body together. She was one of those poor souls who had lost her lover on the eve of her marriage and forevermore mourned him.

When she died, strangers swarmed over her house. At the time of the auc-

tion there had been no one of near enough
kin to take the trouble to go over the
house and put away the little trivial
effects of the dead which no casual eye
should ever see, and so there was un-
covered before the gaping town row after row of empty bottles of complexion
bleach slightly tinged with pink; people laughed and gossiped and thought
it was very funny. There were others
who frowned, asserting that at her time
of life this woman should have known
better than to spend her few pennies
on such folly; which was all, no doubt,
very wise and true. This poor lady kept
herself young only for herself. I suppose
she did n't want the ghost of her dead
lover to find a wrinkled old woman in
place of the fresh-faced girl he had
loved.

You may be sure that almost all older women who refuse to grow old gracefully reveal some tragedy in these mistaken efforts which should cause younger people to be sorry. After all, it is growing old gracefully in the spirit that counts, and it seems to me more important as we advance in years that our spirits should be sweetened, and that we should be kinder in our outlook upon life, and that we should fight against the egotism of age, than that we should dress in a way to proclaim our years.

Perhaps my turning away from my looking - glass, and all my self - consciousness and rebellion at the advancing traces of years, are a greater sin against the true standard of growing old gracefully than those who can trick themselves into a belief that they look young and try naïvely to trick others.

When a young woman criticizes an older for these foibles, I do not think she is preparing herself in her heart to grow old gracefully, and yet all of us are preparing every day for what sort of old age we are going to pass. The question of growing old as one should is a very deep one. It is n't a matter of clothes; it is as deep as life itself.

When I was young I can remember certain older people whose passing through a room seemed to me like a benediction. There was one elderly relative of mine — a woman who had never married — with whom I used to pass afternoons. I don't think that I ever told her one of my troubles, great or small, but her very presence was so sweet, so gallant, so up-standing, and, withal, humorous, — so like a perpetual sermon to me, — that I used to come from her feeling as though I had drunk of the spring of life; and yet her life had been difficult. Report said she had turned her face from the marriage she desired to take care of an exacting mother; she had brought up a brood of younger brothers and sisters, and always she had fought against poverty, and, unflinching, faced loneliness as the years advanced. She, if you like, had grown old gracefully, and yet, had she insisted on dressing in scarlet and painting her cheeks to match her gown, she would have grown old no less gracefully, it seems to me.

I remember another time, when I was hurrying home to the bedside of a sick child, that my companion in the car was an old man, and as we traveled together many hours, he told me the story of his life. To hear him speak of his wife, who had died some years before, was a thing that made one believe in mankind; to hear him speak in a simple, refreshing way of his faith would make one, doubting, believe in God. He himself was fighting for the life of a son who had been stricken with consumption, but was winning in the fight. His brave talk and his loving attitude of mind poured I know not what strength into my own faltering spirit, and enabled me to go to the nursing that was before me with an unflinching heart, though he knew nothing of my trouble.

As I grow older, I see examples

here and there of lovely and inspiring old age, and I pray that I may
grow old gracefully in some image
like that.

The Riverside Press
CAMBRIDGE · MASSACHUSETTS
U · S · A

THE CORNER OF
HARLEY STREET

Being some familiar correspondence of

PETER HARDING, M.D.

"A fair criticism, a complete defence, and some high praise of the doctoring trade." — *London Punch*.

"The book is ripe, well written, thoughtful, piquant and highly human. A thread of romance runs happily through it." — *Chicago Record-Herald*.

"There is nothing upon which the genial Dr. Harding has not something to say that is worth listening to." — *London Daily Mail*.

"The publishers of 'The Corner of Harley Street' are really justified in comparing these critical papers with Dr. Holmes' 'The Autocrat of the Breakfast Table.' . . . They are charmingly discursive, often witty, and always full of a genial sympathy with humanity and the significant facts of life." — *The Outlook*.

$1.25 *net*. Postage 11 cents.

HOUGHTON
MIFFLIN
COMPANY

BOSTON
AND
NEW YORK

QUEED

By HENRY SYDNOR HARRISON

" Just what a novel should be. Queed is an original and delightful personality that will never vanish from the memory." — *Transcript.*

."A sympathetic picture of the development of the New South, with one of the gayest, brightest, bravest daughters for heroine." — *The Living Age.*

" Queed is quite the quaintest, most whimsical sort of a personage imaginable." — *Pasadena Daily News.*

" Queed is an intensely human story, original, stimulating, permeated by a delightful humor and a charming spirit." — *New Orleans Picayune.*

With frontispiece. $1.35 *net.* Postpaid, $1.47

HOUGHTON
MIFFLIN
COMPANY

BOSTON
AND
NEW YORK

THE LONG ROLL

By MARY JOHNSTON

"The greatest novel of the Civil War. . . . No one should omit reading it."—*Cleveland Plain Dealer*.

"Other writers have made us see the details of battles, but few have given so complete and sympathetic an account of what war means to all those directly affected. . . . One who reads this book will always have a more sympathetic understanding of what the war was to the South."— *Charlotte Observer*.

" 'The Long Roll ' steps at one stride into the front rank of American fiction. . . . No other novel of the American Civil War approaches it in power. . . . It is an Iliad of great and massive fighting."— *New York Evening Mail*.

"Her spirit is large and fine, free from sectional bitterness, though loyally Virginian in viewpoint. . . . It is a great book that she has written."— *Chicago Record-Herald*.

Illustrated in color. $1.40 *net*. Postpaid $1.54

HOUGHTON
MIFFLIN
COMPANY

BOSTON
AND
NEW YORK

SCOTTIE AND HIS LADY

By MARGARET MORSE

"The story of a handsome, intelligent collie dog. It is entertainingly and sympathetically told, and sure of the absorbed interest of every young lover of animals." — *Chicago Daily News.*

"Instantly deserves a place with Richard Harding Davis's 'Bar Sinister,' Alfred Ollivant's 'Bob, Son of Battle,' and Jack London's 'Call of the Wild.'" — *Boston Transcript.*

"A delightful love story is woven in with the joys and trials of Scottie, who finds perfect satisfaction in the happy culmination of the romance of his lady." — *Chicago Record-Herald.*

Illustrated by H. M. Brett.
12mo, $1.10 *net.*   Postage 11 cents.

HOUGHTON
MIFFLIN
COMPANY

BOSTON
AND
NEW YORK

THE MEDDLINGS OF EVE

By WILLIAM J. HOPKINS

" Mr. Hopkins is a true humorist. His distinction is to have found a new literary field and to have peopled it with original and living characters that may not unjustly give him claim to rank with the best of our living American writers." — *Boston Transcript.*

"Humor, dignity, and most perfect human love shine out in these charming stories." — *The Outlook.*

"Mr. Hopkins is a master of the sort of quiet humor which makes the charm of these stories." — *Congregationalist.*

"A story full of subtle situations . . . a delightful volume." — *San Francisco Chronicle.*

Tall 12mo, $1.00 *net.* Postage 9 cents.

HOUGHTON
MIFFLIN
COMPANY

BOSTON
AND
NEW YORK

WHEN SHE CAME HOME FROM COLLEGE

By MARIAN K. HURD and JEAN B. WILSON

"An especially natural and breezy college girl's story." — *Baltimore Sun.*

"A book of vital interest to the college girl, to her family, and to all who are concerned directly or indirectly in college education for girls."

Hartford Courant.

"Deserves high commendation, both for its lessons of wisdom, and the wholesome satire of its fun — a book with much charm." — *Chicago Evening Post.*

"Not for a long while have we read such a refreshing narrative as this." — *Literary Digest.*

Illustrated. 12mo, $1.15 *net.* Postage 10 cents.

HOUGHTON
MIFFLIN
COMPANY

BOSTON
AND
NEW YORK

JOHN WINTERBOURNE'S FAMILY

By ALICE BROWN

"A delightful and unusual story. The manner in which the hero's male solitude is invaded and set right is amusing and eccentric enough to have been devised by the late Frank Stockton. It is a story that is well worth reading." — *New York Sun.*

"Is to be counted among the best novels of this entertaining writer . . . written with a skilful and delicate touch." — *Springfield Republican.*

"In its literary graces, in its portrayal of characters that are never commonplace though genuinely human, and in its development of a singular social situation, the book is one to give delight." — *Philadelphia Press.*

12mo, $1.35 *net.* Postage 13 cents.

HOUGHTON
MIFFLIN
COMPANY

BOSTON
AND
NEW YORK

3926

Trieste Publishing has a massive catalogue of classic book titles. Our aim is to provide readers with the highest quality reproductions of fiction and non-fiction literature that has stood the test of time. The many thousands of books in our collection have been sourced from libraries and private collections around the world.

The titles that Trieste Publishing has chosen to be part of the collection have been scanned to simulate the original. Our readers see the books the same way that their first readers did decades or a hundred or more years ago. Books from that period are often spoiled by imperfections that did not exist in the original. Imperfections could be in the form of blurred text, photographs, or missing pages. It is highly unlikely that this would occur with one of our books. Our extensive quality control ensures that the readers of Trieste Publishing's books will be delighted with their purchase. Our staff has thoroughly reviewed every page of all the books in the collection, repairing, or if necessary, rejecting titles that are not of the highest quality. This process ensures that the reader of one of Trieste Publishing's titles receives a volume that faithfully reproduces the original, and to the maximum degree possible, gives them the experience of owning the original work.

We pride ourselves on not only creating a pathway to an extensive reservoir of books of the finest quality, but also providing value to every one of our readers. Generally, Trieste books are purchased singly - on demand, however they may also be purchased in bulk. Readers interested in bulk purchases are invited to contact us directly to enquire about our tailored bulk rates. Email: customerservice@triestepublishing.com

You May Also Like

Local Taxation and the Rating of Machinery.
A Report on the Rating of Machinery, with
All the Decided Cases Thereon,
from 1783 down to the Present Time,
Including the Short-Hand Writer's Notes of
the Special Case, Arguments, and Judgment

Thos. Fenwick Hedley

ISBN: 9780649638468
Paperback: 248 pages
Dimensions: 6.14 x 0.52 x 9.21 inches
Language: eng

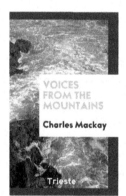

Voices from the Mountains

Charles Mackay

ISBN: 9780649730360
Paperback: 140 pages
Dimensions: 5.25 x 0.30 x 8.0 inches
Language: eng

www.triestepublishing.com

You May Also Like

Results of Astronomical Observations Made at the Sydney Observatory, New South Wales, in the Years 1877 and 1878

H. C. Russell

ISBN: 9780649692613
Paperback: 120 pages
Dimensions: 6.14 x 0.25 x 9.21 inches
Language: eng

War Poems, 1898

California Club & Irving M. Scott

ISBN: 9780649731213
Paperback: 160 pages
Dimensions: 6.14 x 0.34 x 9.21 inches
Language: eng

You May Also Like

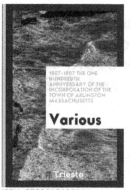

1807-1907 The One Hundredth Anniversary of the incorporation of the Town of Arlington Massachusetts

Various

ISBN: 9780649420544
Paperback: 108 pages
Dimensions: 6.14 x 0.22 x 9.21 inches
Language: eng

Biennial report of the Board of State Harbor Commissioners, for the two fiscal years commencing July 1, 1890, and ending June 30, 1892

Various

ISBN: 9780649194292
Paperback: 44 pages
Dimensions: 6.14 x 0.09 x 9.21 inches
Language: eng

www.triestepublishing.com

You May Also Like

ISBN: 9780649199693
Paperback: 48 pages
Dimensions: 6.14 x 0.10 x 9.21 inches
Language: eng

Biennial report of the Board of State Harbor Commissioners for the two fisca years. Commeneing July 1, 1884, and Ending June 30, 1886

Various

ISBN: 9780649196395
Paperback: 44 pages
Dimensions: 6.14 x 0.09 x 9.21 inches
Language: eng

Biennial report of the Board of state commissioners, for the two fiscal years, commencing July 1, 1890, and ending June 30, 1892

Various

Find more of our titles on our website. We have a selection of thousands of titles that will interest you. Please visit

www.triestepublishing.com

Lightning Source UK Ltd.
Milton Keynes UK
UKOW01f1329231017
311488UK00017B/3681/P